The Outdoor Grill Cookbook

The Outdoor Grill Cookbook

Previously Published as *The Hungry Man's Outdoor Grill Cookbook*
and *The Master Chef's Outdoor Grill Cookbook*

by the Staff Home Economists
Culinary Arts Institute
MELANIE DE PROFT,
Director

GROSSET & DUNLAP
A NATIONAL GENERAL COMPANY
Publishers · New York

A Castle Books, Inc. Edition
Distributed To The Trade
By Book Sales, Inc.

Contents

Introduction

Go West, where whole steers were roasted over glowing coals and devoured at one sitting.

"Go South, to the political conclaves where candidates provided sheep, beeves, suckling pigs with sweet potatoes and corn for their voters.

"Go East, to the shore and the clambake.

"Go North, to the campsites where trout jumped out of the brook into the frying pan."

This was the call a generation or two ago. Today you and your friends go to the backyard, beach and byways to your own grill party or cookout.

Outdoor cooking is something for everyone—men, women and teenagers—to enjoy doing today. To help you start this new adventure —or renew an old familiar one—here are the *Mixin's of a Good Cookout*.

First things first and a *grill* is an essential. There are all types to fit all pocketbooks and all wants—portable ones that may be moved anywhere and those so large they should remain at home in the backyard. Choose one that fulfills your special need. Look around, shop wisely.

To cook you must have *heat*—and here, please take heed. A fire can grill to perfection or burn to a crisp. "A little wind and a lot of patience" should hang invisibly over your grill when you build your cooking fire.

Charcoal lumps or briquets are the types of *fuel* preferred by the experts. At times you may want to use a hard wood or fruit wood such as apple or hickory chips. Dampened hickory chips tossed on a charcoal fire just before the meat is placed on the grill is an added flavor touch. Soft woods like pine give foods a tarry soot coating and do not produce a satisfactory bed of coals.

To build a cooking fire—Start with a good bed of charcoal, 2 to 3 inches deep. (It should last the entire cooking period.) Sprinkle Charcolite or other charcoal lighters over and ignite. You'll find plenty to keep you busy while you wait for the coals to burn to a gray color with a ruddy glow underneath. This is your cooking fire which gives a hot, sustained, glowing heat. Allow 30 minutes for your fire to become a bed of coals ready for grilling.

Another way to start the fire is by beginning the bed with a small amount of paper and kindling. Add a small amount of charcoal and when it is burning, build the entire bed as directed.

To control heat—The distance from the top of the coals to the food helps determine the degree of heat. More distance means less heat and slower grilling. Some grills have adjustable fireboxes that can raise or lower the bed of coals.

Hoods that are built on the back of some

grills intensify the heat. Shorten cooking times slightly if using such a grill.

TIMING OF COOKING PERIODS WILL VARY WITH SIZE OF FIREBOX, DEGREE OF HEAT, AMOUNT AND DIRECTION OF WIND AND TYPE OF GRILL USED. TIMINGS AND DISTANCES GIVEN IN THIS BOOK ARE ONLY GUIDES.

During grilling, when flare-ups occur (usually just at the start of cooking as a result of fat dripping onto the coals), douse flames with a small amount of water. Careful aim with a basting tube filled with water, or a water pistol, controls most blaze-ups.

There is a wide variety of *grill equipment* available. Some items are necessary, some are useful additions and others are merely colorful gadgets.

AN APRON that is big enough to keep grease spatters and soot from your favorite sport clothes.

ASBESTOS OR WELL-PADDED GLOVES prevent cooked hands. It's cooked food that you are aiming at. Remember these are hot, live coals that you are grilling over.

These items are necessary to make full use of your grill.

LONG-HANDLED HAND TOOLS. These include forks, spoons, turners, tongs and basting brushes.. One of each is sufficient to start with. Basting brushes can be the pastry brush from the kitchen or a wooden stick with celery and sage leaves tied to it.

SHARP KNIVES. These are for carving and testing doneness of meat.

A TABLE or working space. A card table with steady legs or a portable picnic table fills the bill for large affairs. Some grills have extra space provided. When camping out, a clean, flat rock doubles nicely.

PAPER TOWELS and a place to dispose of "throw-aways."

Useful additions to your equipment, such as these, lead you on to new culinary skills.

A CARVING BOARD.

A BASTING TUBE to control flare-ups.

A STEAK BROILER or basket steak broiler. They look very much like the old-fashioned bread toasters. Small or extra-tender foods and many large cuts of meat are more easily turned with these.

A SKILLET with a long handle. Fried foods are better-than-ever when done on the grill.

ONE HUGE KETTLE—that holds everything and anything.

KEBAB SKEWERS which are long thin pieces of metal. You used the green stick variety during your youngest years.

A SPIT ATTACHMENT on your grill. Many grills have the hand-propelled type, but an electric rotary spit is a convenience that any gourmet will insist upon.

DRIP PANS—used when basting roasts and large pieces of meat done on the spit.

LARGE COFFEE POT.

ICE CHEST—for carrying milk, butter, vegetables, fruit—those things you want to keep cool and fresh till serving time.

ICE CREAM FREEZER—whether you put in a plug or turn the crank yourself—you'll always have fun making Freezer Ice Cream.

BARBECUE THERMOMETER—is your best guide to accurate roasting. Insert thermometer into meat or poultry at an angle so it will not touch bone or spit. Do not let it hit hood, drip pan, or coals.

Cooking methods are:

GRILLING—many foods that can be broiled or fried in the kitchen can be grilled outside. Skillets and shish kebab skewers give versatility to your cooking. Recipes are given in this book for both.

SPIT ROASTING—many meats and poultry which can be roasted in the kitchen oven adapt well to the spit. To shorten spit roasting time (especially when a hand-propelled-type spit is used), food may be precooked in oven before placing on spit.

When *serving*, plan to use from-the-hand foods. But for those spectacular specialties of yours, use: colorful tableware—plastic, wood, paper; large napkins or tablecloths—preferably paper or bright-colored cotton; picnic tables—large and sturdy to withstand the abundance of food needed to satisfy outdoor appetites.

Now, combine all these *Mixin's* and place in the backyard, picnic ground or on the beach. The world of outdoor grilling is yours for the trying.

Outdoor Menu

Charcoal Broiled Steak

Mix and set aside . . .

> 1 *tablespoon salt*
> 2 *teaspoons monosodium glutamate*
> ¼ *teaspoon freshly ground pepper*

Rub . . .

> 4 *lbs. beef steaks, such as sirloin, porter-house, tenderloin, T-bone or rib, cut 1½ in. thick*

with cut side of . . .

> 1 *clove garlic*

Lightly grease grill with . . .

> *Cooking oil or olive oil*

Place steaks on grill about 3 in. from coals. Grill about 6 min., or until first side is browned. Turn with tongs and sprinkle half of seasoning mixture over top of steaks. Grill second side about 6 min., or until done. To test doneness, slit meat near bone and note color of meat.

Season second side of steaks. Remove from grill to serving plates.

Pour over them . . .

¼ cup melted butter

If you like, serve commercial steak sauce with steaks.

Eat promptly! 4 servings.

—Gourmet's Steak

Soften ¼ lb. Blue cheese and spread on steaks after turning.

—Saucy Steak

During grilling baste steaks with soy sauce or a favorite commercial steak sauce. Serve steaming hot with gobs of butter.

—Marinade School Steak

Place steaks in shallow pan. Pour over them 1½ cups olive oil with seasonings and juice of one lemon. Let stand about 2 hrs. in refrigerator, turning occasionally. When ready to grill remove from marinade.

—One-Inch Steaks

Steaks about 1 in. thick will require less time to grill (about 4 min. on each side). Grill about 3 in. from coals.

—Strip or Club Steaks

Grill strip or club steaks about 4 min. on each side 3 in. from coals. Season and let butter melt over top.

Chef's Notes

1. If dripping fat causes a flare-up, douse the flame with a small amount of water. A basting tube or water pistol may be used for this.

2. Grill steaks rare. But for those few who like theirs medium done, grill their steaks a moment or so longer on each side.

3. *Rocky Mountain Cobbler*—A wedge of apple pie placed in a tin cup, with thick rich cream poured over it is an outdoor feast finale.

—Cubed Steaks

Have meat dealer cube round, arm, blade or flank steak. Grill about 3 in. from coals about 15 min., total grilling time. Season steaks and pour melted butter over top.

—Sandwich Steaks

Have meat dealer prepare Sandwich Steaks by cutting beef tenderloin into pieces and flattening them. Grill 3 in. from coals about 3 min. on each side.

Tossed Salad

All the ingredients for this salad can be prepared ahead of time and then chilled in the refrigerator. When eating-time comes, all you have to do is get them from the refrigerator and toss them together

Wash in cold water and drain well . . .
   1 *head of lettuce*
Tear into bite-size pieces. Wash gently, but thoroughly, in cold water and drain well . . .
   1 *bunch water cress*
Cut into short sprays. Place greens in plastic bag and chill. Rub wooden salad bowl with cut side of . . .
   1 *clove garlic*
Just before serving toss greens lightly in bowl with . . .
   ⅓ *cup French Dressing*
Cut into serving-size pieces . . .
   2 *firm tomatoes*
   1 *ripe avocado, peeled*
Toss slightly with greens. Scatter on top . . .
   2 *hard-cooked eggs (page 91) cut into quarters*
   Pitted colossal ripe olives
4 servings.

—Tossed Salad Garnishes
Strips of carrots, green and sweet red peppers, spears of celery, raw cauliflowerets, cheese slivers, thin slices of cucumber, buds of radishes and onions—all can be skillfully tucked into your Tossed Salad.
The time of year, garden availability, guests' preference and your likes help to determine your choices.

French Dressing

Combine in a bowl or screw-top jar . . .

> 1 *tablespoon sugar*
> 1 *teaspoon dry mustard*
> 1 *teaspoon paprika*
> 1 *teaspoon salt*
> ¼ *teaspoon celery seed*
> ¾ *cup salad or olive oil*
> ¼ *cup mild or wine vinegar or lemon juice*

Beat or shake until blended. Add . . .

> 1 *clove garlic*

Store, covered, in refrigerator. When ready to use, shake and remove garlic. About 1 cup dressing.

—Roquefort French Dressing

Combine ½ cup French Dressing with 1 oz. Roquefort or Blue cheese, crumbled. Toss with greens.

Outdoor Menu

Grilled Chicken
Lemon Basting Sauce   Fried Mushrooms
Tomato Wedges in Tossed Greens
French Rolls (54)
Bakery Shortcakes with Berries
Beverage

Grilled Chicken

Clean, rinse and dry with absorbent paper . . .

*2 broiler chickens, 1 to 1½ lbs. each,
ready-to-cook weight*

Split each chicken in half lengthwise. If chickens are frozen, thaw according to directions on package. Crack joints of drumsticks, hips and wings so chickens can be kept flat during grilling. Skewer legs and wings to bodies. Brush chickens with . . .

Lemon Basting Sauce (See p. 8)

Place chickens on greased portion of grill or in greased steak broiler. Grill cut-side down 3 in. from coals. Turn chickens every 5 min. to brown and cook evenly. Brush frequently with sauce.

Grill about 20 min. (depending on size of chickens), or until chickens test done. They are done when meat on thickest part of drumstick cuts easily and no pink color shows.

Serve a half, with remaining sauce, to each of your guests. They will thoroughly enjoy this feast. 4 servings.

Chef's Notes

1. When crisp chicken is piled high in a basket and set near a stack of large paper napkins, it's easy to help one's self—often.

2. *Tossed Greens*—Choose fresh greens from your garden. Wash them well, shake off excess water and turn into a big salad bowl. Place bowl in a large plastic bag and set in refrigerator to chill.

3. *Tomato Wedges*—Strike a note of color in your salad with the addition of ripe red tomato wedges. When ready to serve, drizzle French dressing over the salad and toss lightly together.

—Fried Chicken

Disjoint into serving-size pieces fryer chickens, about 2½ lbs. each, ready-to-cook weight. Quickly rinse pieces in cold water and dry. For added flavor, if you like, dip and turn pieces of chicken in a deep bowl of buttermilk, covering each piece evenly. Drain well on absorbent paper.

Put in a paper bag a mixture of 1 cup flour, 1½ teaspoons salt, ½ teaspoon monosodium glutamate and ½ teaspoon pepper. To coat chicken evenly, shake 2 or 3 pieces at a time in the bag.

Heat enough fat in a large heavy deep iron skillet to make a layer at least ½ in. deep. Starting with thickest pieces, fry chicken on both sides until golden brown and tender. The result is wonderful—watch the group gather.

7

Lemon Basting Sauce

Melt . . .

> *¾ cup butter*

Mix and stir into melted butter . . .

> *2 teaspoons paprika*
> *1 teaspoon sugar*
> *1 teaspoon salt*
> *½ teaspoon black pepper*
> *¼ teaspoon dry mustard*
> > *Few grains cayenne pepper*

Blend in thoroughly . . .

> *½ cup lemon juice*
> *½ cup hot water*
> > *Few drops tabasco sauce*

Baste chicken frequently with sauce during grilling. If you wish, add 2 tablespoons grated onion to the sauce. About 1½ cups sauce.

Fried Mushrooms

Wipe with a damp cloth and cut off tips of stems from . . .

> *12 large mushrooms*

Carefully pull caps from stems. Heat in skillet . . .

> *⅓ cup butter*

Add mushroom caps and stems to skillet. Cook slowly, stirring gently until lightly browned. Serve piping hot with the chicken. 4 servings.

Outdoor Menu

Ground Meat in Barbecue Sauce
Grilled Buns
Potato Chips   Roast Corn   Relishes
Apple Turnovers
Beverage

Ground Meat in Barbecue Sauce

Barbecue Sauce—Preparing this in advance will save you time.

Combine in pint jar . . .

  1 *cup ketchup*
  ½ *cup water*
  2 *tablespoons sugar*
  2 *tablespoons prepared mustard*
  2 *tablespoons vinegar*
  2 *teaspoons Worcestershire sauce*

To prepare meat, heat in skillet . . .

  2 *tablespoons butter*

Add and cook until transparent . . .

  1 *cup chopped onion*

Stir in . . .

  2 *lbs. ground beef, crumbled*
  2 *teaspoons salt*
  ½ *teaspoon monosodium glutamate*
  ½ *teaspoon pepper*

When meat is browned, stir in sauce. Place skillet on back of grill and cook slowly about 15 min. Guests themselves can spoon the meat and sauce into buttered buns. Have plates ready for this; it's juicy. 4 to 6 servings.

—Beef or Pork in Barbecue Sauce
Substitute slices of cooked beef or pork for ground meat. Heat slices in Barbecue Sauce. Serve on buns.

Roast Corn

Loosen husks only enough to remove silks and blemishes from ears of . . .

> *Garden-fresh corn (you'll be the best judge of quantity)*

Dip ears in deep pail of water. Shake well. Rewrap husks around corn. Plunge in water again and let stand until husks are soaked. Place ears

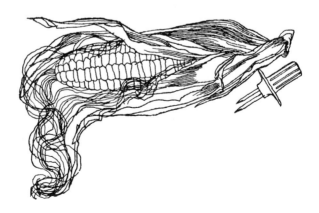

Chef's Notes

1. Select corn with long stem ends—they'll make handling and turning easier. Allow stem ends to extend beyond end of grill.

2. *Grilled Buns*—A few minutes before serving time, slice bakery buns, butter; place, cut-side down, on grill and toast. Watch them closely.

3. This is a finger meal. Let everyone serve himself from the grill. A second round of buns and corn can be toasting and roasting while round one disappears.

4. *Apple Turnovers*—Buy 'em.

on grill over hot coals. Roast, turning often, until tender (about 15 min.). Husk and serve.

—Butter Roasted Corn

Remove husks, silks and any blemishes from corn. For each ear of corn to be served, cream 1 tablespoon butter until softened. Work in 1 teaspoon minced parsley, ¼ teaspoon salt and dash of paprika. Spread on corn. Wrap each ear loosely in aluminum foil, sealing carefully. Place on grill over hot coals. Roast about 15 min., turning frequently. Partially unwrap and serve corn in the foil.

Asbestos gloves are one of the barbecuer's best friends—wear them regularly

Outdoor Menu

Fresh Pineapple Cubes
Grilled Hamburgers   Toasted Buns
Tomato and Onion Slices As You Like 'Em
Roast Corn (10)   Melted Butter
Freezer Ice Cream
Beverage

Grilled Hamburger

Mix—lightly though . . .

2 lbs. ground beef
2 teaspoons salt
1 teaspoon monosodium glutamate
¼ teaspoon pepper

Shape into 4 or 6 patties. Chef—you're the judge, for some like them thick, some slightly thinner. Place patties in greased steak broiler. Grill about 5 in. from coals. Cook about 4 min. on one side. Turn and brush with . . .

Melted butter

Brown second side; don't forget to brush this side with melted butter, too. Serve the hamburgers hot in toasted buns.

For variety, mix in one or a combination of these with the seasonings—but go easy on the hot ones . . .

½ cup chopped onion
¼ cup chopped green pepper or olives
¼ cup ketchup or chili sauce
5-oz. can mushrooms, drained and chopped

Chef's Notes

1. Ground beef should not be too fat, but if too lean, it will crumble and fall through the grill.

2. Handle ground meat gently; pat into shape—do not press.

3. For that special outdoor flavor, toss moistened hickory chips or sawdust on coals a few minutes before meat is put on grill

4. *Onion Slices*—Cut onion slices thick or thin. Eat them raw, fry in butter or grill with hamburgers.

1 *clove garlic, finely chopped*
1 *tablespoon pickle relish, prepared*
    mustard or Worcestershire sauce
2 *teaspoons horseradish*
1 *teaspoon chili powder, dry mustard,*
    garlic or onion salt

4 to 6 hamburgers.

—Grilled Lamb-Burgers

Substitute ground lamb for beef and mix with seasonings. You might add ¼ teaspoon dill seed or 2 tablespoons chopped mint leaves if you have an extra moment.

—Hamburgers à la Barbecue Sauce

Brush patties with Barbecue Sauce (see Sauce-Painted Spareribs, page 64) before, during and after grilling.

Smoke and guests do not blend well. Remember to place your portable grill so that smoke will blow away from them

—Chef-with-the-Skillet Burgers

Melt butter in a skillet. Add the patties and brown just right on each side.

TOASTED BUNS

Cut buns into halves and brush cut side with melted butter. Place on grill and toast cut side. Add more melted butter and serve the buns hot. For extra crispness, toast uncut side a moment before serving.

Freezer Ice Cream

Wash and scald cover, container and dasher of a 2-qt. ice cream freezer. Chill them thoroughly before using. Mix until sugar is dissolved . . .

> 1½ qts. cream
> 1 cup sugar
> 3 tablespoons vanilla
> Dash of salt

Fill chilled container not more than two-thirds full with ice cream mixture. Cover tightly. Set into freezer tub. (For electric freezer, follow manufacturer's directions.) Fill tub with alternate layers of . . .

> 8 parts crushed ice
> 1 part rock salt

Turn handle slowly 5 min. Turn rapidly until handle becomes difficult to turn (about 15 min.). Wipe lid well and remove dasher. Pack down ice cream and cover with waxed paper. Put lid again on top and fill opening for dasher with cork. Repack freezer in ice using . . .

4 parts ice
1 part rock salt

Cover with heavy paper or cloth. Plan to have ice cream prepared 1 to 2 hrs. before dessert time. It's best when allowed to ripen. About 2 qts. ice cream.

—Peach or Strawberry Ice Cream

Stir in a mixture of 1 tablespoon lemon juice and 3 cups mashed, sweetened peaches or strawberries before freezing. Omit vanilla.

—Chocolate Ice Cream

Heat 3 sq. (3 oz.) unsweetened chocolate until melted in cream over simmering water. Increase sugar to 1¾ cups. Beat sugar and salt into chocolate mixture with rotary beater. Cool. Add vanilla and chill. Freeze as in Freezer Ice Cream.

—Nut Brittle Ice Cream

Crush ½ lb. nut brittle and stir into cream mixture for Freezer Ice Cream just before freezing. Almond, pecan and peanut brittle give equally good results.

Outdoor Menu

Iced Fruit Juice
Cheeseburgers   Relish Buns
Potato Chips   Vegetable Kebabs
Ice Cream Cones
Beverage

Cheese Burgers

Mix . . .

>1 *egg, beaten*
>1 *tablespoon Worcestershire sauce or*
>   *prepared mustard*
>1 *teaspoon salt*
>1 *teaspoon monosodium glutamate*
>1 *teaspoon onion salt or hickory-*
>   *smoked salt*
>¼ *teaspoon pepper*

Mix in with a light touch . . .

>2 *lbs. ground beef*

Better under than over on the seasonings—that's enough for now. Shape the hamburgers to the size of your buns, 4 to 6 of them. Brush burgers with . . .

>*Melted butter*

Place in greased steak broiler. Grill 3 in. from coals about 6 min. Turn to brown second side and brush again with butter. Grill second side about 6 min. After 4 min., top browned side with . . .

>*Cheddar cheese slice*

Chef's Notes

1. *Iced Fruit Juice*—Start off with fruit juice, made ice-cold with lemon sherbet or crushed ice, and served from a thermos. Apricot, pineapple, or cranberry juice are all fine beginners.

2. *Relish Buns*—Cut buns in halves and grill them until lightly browned. Then spread with butter and pickle relish before popping in your special cheeseburgers.

3. No need for spoons or dishes with ice cream cone desserts. If there's more than one flavor of ice cream you can have rainbow-deckers.

As second side browns, the golden cheese will melt over the burger. They will be done so quickly that you're likely to get a genius rating. Serve the burgers pronto in toasted buns.

Next time try adding chopped dill pickle, chives, toasted nuts, chopped mushrooms or sesame seed to the meat mixture. They're good with cheese.

—Sandwich-Style Hamburgers

Make twice as many patties by making them thinner. Spread half the patties with a softened cheese, such as a cheese spread or a smoked cheese; top with remaining patties, press edges together and grill. Or, spread with a mixture of ½ teaspoon olive oil and 2 teaspoons Roquefort or Blue cheese.

You can also place a thin slice of Cheddar cheese between the patties.

—Cheesey-Burgers

Mix 1 cup (about 4 oz.) grated Cheddar or Swiss cheese with the ground beef mixture. Grill as usual.

—Blue Cheese-Burgers

Omit Worcestershire sauce or prepared mustard in meat mixture. Mix ¼ cup (about 2 oz.) Blue or Roquefort cheese, crumbled, with 1 tablespoon each of mayonnaise and softened butter, 1½ teaspoons Worcestershire sauce and ¼ teaspoon dry mustard. Just before the hamburgers are done on second side, spread this over the top of each. The heat will melt it slightly.

—Surprise Hamburgers

Mold the hamburger mixture around cubes of Cheddar or Swiss cheese. Grill the same as usual. The soft cheese centers will be a pleasant surprise.

For really fast cheese-flavored burgers, sprinkle browned burgers with grated Parmesan cheese just before serving.

Vegetable Kebabs

While you prepare the meat, here's a chance for the guests to make and cook their own vegetable kebabs.

Cook potatoes and onions in advance. Have

them ready in bowls with the other vegetables. To make the kebabs all your guests have to do with the vegetables is thread them on a skewer.

As you gain skill you will want to experiment with different vegetable combinations of your own, but those listed here can be a beginning. Here's how to prepare them:

Wash, pare and cook, covered, in boiling salted water to cover . . .

6 *small potatoes*

Cook about 15 min., or until tender. Wash, peel and cook, uncovered in boiling salted water to cover . . .

6 *small onions*

Cook about 10 min., or until tender. Or, use canned potatoes and onions to eliminate cooking. Meanwhile, wipe with a damp cloth and cut off stem ends from . . .

12 *large mushrooms*

Wrap each mushroom cap in . . .

Bacon

Set aside. Wash, remove pulp and cut into 12 1-in. squares . . .

Green pepper

Drain potatoes and onions; arrange on 6 skewers with the mushroom caps and green pepper squares. With each vegetable added to the skewer, appetites too will lengthen. Brush the vegetables with French Dressing (page 5) or melted butter. Grill until lightly browned, turning often for even browning. Baste frequently.

During last 3 to 5 min. of grilling, add to each skewer . . .

1 *small tomato*

Sprinkle kebabs with a mixture of . . .

1 *teaspoon salt*
¼ *teaspoon monosodium glutamate*
⅛ *teaspoon pepper*

Serve them hot. 6 kebabs.

—Sweet Potato Kebabs

Substitute sweet potatoes for white potatoes. Do not peel them until after cooking. Cook about 25 min., or just until tender. Alternate pieces on skewer with pineapple cubes and apple wedges. Provide some marshmallows to go on the skewers for a "sweet tooth" crowd. Marshmallows should be added last, about 1 min. before serving.

—Vegetable Variations

Wash, pare and cut 1 medium-size (about 1 lb.) eggplant into 1½-in. cubes. Summer squash or zucchini may also be pared and cut for the skewers.

**Nothing is worse than chilled meat. Serve it
quickly when it is done**

Outdoor Menu

Beef Roast on a Spit

Select...

5-lb. rolled and boned rib beef roast

Have a good layer of fat around the outside of roast or an additional layer of suet around it.

Secure meat on spit. Insert barbecue thermometer and place spit in position. Put drip pan under meat to catch drippings. Start motor and roast meat until desired doneness. Allow 15-18 min. per lb. for rare meat (140°F), 20-25 min. per lb. for medium (160°F), and 30-35 min. per lb. (170°F) for well done. (Without a thermometer, test roast for doneness by cutting a slit in meat and noting color.) When using a hand-propelled-type spit, turn meat as it sears, then turn about every 10 min. during roasting.

Baste roast frequently with drippings, butter, or Barbecue Sauce (see Sauce-Painted Spareribs, p. 64).

Carve roast; season with salt and pepper. 8 to 10 servings.

For additional flavor, cut slits in meat before

roasting and insert slivers of onion or garlic. Then roast. A hood on the grill insures thorough cooking.

Grilled Onions

Leave dry outside skins on . . .

Spanish or Bermuda onions, at least one for each guest

Wet each thoroughly. Place on grill while cooking meat. Roll onions around occasionally. They are done when black on the outside and soft and creamy on the inside (about 50 min.).

Vegetable Nibblers

Chill any of the following and arrange on trays or in bowls. Crushed ice or ice cubes added to the bowl will keep the nibblers crisp.

Tomato wedges
Carrot straws, sticks or curls
Radish roses
Kohlrabi strips
Cucumber slices
Celery sticks
Stuffed celery
Cauliflowerets
Scallions
Green pepper strips
Lettuce or celery hearts

Green, ripe and stuffed olives, cocktail onions

Chef's Notes

1. A roast that is rolled insures even cooking and easy placing on spit.

2. Rolled roasts are an interesting way to serve a large number of people.

3. *Tomato Consommé*—Heat contents of cans of condensed consommé and tomato juice together. This can be kept warm in the warming pots until serving time.

4. *Cantaloupe with Blueberries*—This not only makes a pretty picture but also "pretty" good eating.

and pickles scattered about the trays will add color and flavor interest.

Place shakers of salt nearby so guests can help themselves.

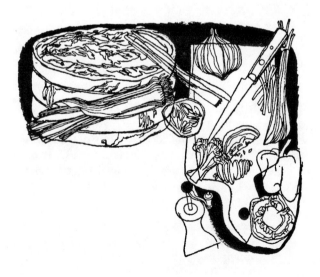

Outdoor Menu

Grilled Fish Steak   Cucumber Sauce
Hashed Brown Potatoes
Broccoli (92)
Plums   Cookies
Beverage

Grilled Fish Steak

Purchase salmon, halibut or swordfish steaks about ¾ in. thick. Allow 1 medium-size steak for each guest.

Combine in shallow dish . . .

½ cup cooking oil
¼ cup lemon juice

Place in dish . . .

4 fish steaks

Cover lightly with waxed paper. Let stand about 30 min., turning and basting each steak frequently. Drain fish slightly and place in greased steak broiler. Grill about 3 min., 5 in. from coals. Brush with lemon juice mixture or melted butter. Turn fish; brush again. Sprinkle with half a mixture of . . .

4 teaspoons salt
1 teaspoon monosodium glutamate
½ teaspoon pepper

Chef's Notes

1. Frequent basting of fish keeps it from becoming dry.

2. For a gourmet's sauce, substitute whipped cream for half the mayonnaise in each sauce recipe.

3. Bacon drippings are a tasty butter substitute for cooking Hashed Brown Potatoes.

4. Big red, yellow or purple plums with cookies from your bake shop or cookie jar are a simple dessert.

Continue grilling 3 min., or until fish is completely white and flakes easily. Turn and sprinkle with remaining seasonings. Serve them while they're hot. 4 servings.

—Fish Steaks in Foil

Use fish suggested for Grilled Fish Steaks. Sprinkle each steak with seasonings, top with any vegetable such as tomato, onion or egg plant slices, or a combination of vegetables. Wrap each steak loosely in heavy aluminum foil, closing ends of foil with double folds. Place on grill about 3 in. from coals. Grill about 12 min.

—Fried Fish Steaks

Use fish suggested for Grilled Fish Steaks. Sprinkle steaks with seasonings. Cook until golden brown in skillet containing ¼ cup hot butter. Turn steaks carefully with long-handled spatula. Brown second side. Serve at once.

—Fish Fillets

Fish fillets can be grilled, fried or cooked in foil in same way as fish steaks. A wider choice of fish is possible in fillets.

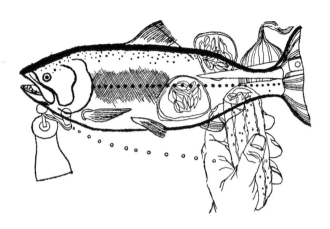

Hash Browned Potatoes

Mix in a bowl (ahead of time, if you wish) . . .

> 3 *cups diced cooked potatoes*
> 2 *tablespoons grated onion*
> 1 *teaspoon salt*
> ½ *teaspoon monosodium glutamate*
> ¼ *teaspoon freshly ground pepper*

Heat in large heavy skillet . . .

> ¼ *cup butter*

Add the potatoes. Press them down firmly with spatula into a 1-in. thick cake. Cook on grill over hot coals until bottom of cake is crusty and browned (about 10 min.). Loosen cake with spatula and flip over in one piece. Brown the second side. Serve with lots of ketchup. 4 servings.

How to Cook Potatoes—Wash and cut into halves . . .

> 4 or 5 *medium-size potatoes*

Place in saucepan with boiling water to cover and add . . .

> 1 *teaspoon salt*

Cover and boil over moderate heat 20 to 30 min., or until potatoes are tender when pierced with a fork. Drain and shake dry over low heat. Peel.

Quick Fish Sauces

Cucumber Sauce

Combine . . .

> 1 *cup mayonnaise*
> 1 *cup chopped cucumber*
> 1 *teaspoon chopped chives*
> 1 *teaspoon chopped onion*
> ½ *teaspoon salt*
> ¼ *teaspoon pepper*
> ⅛ *teaspoon anchovy paste*

Chill. About 2 cups.

Horseradish Sauce

Blend thoroughly . . .

> 1 *cup mayonnaise*
> 3 *tablespoons horseradish, freshly grated or prepared*
> 1 *tablespoon lemon juice*

Chill. About 1¼ cups.

Tartar Sauce
Combine ...

    1 *cup mayonnaise*
    1 *tablespoon chopped pickle*
    1 *tablespoon chopped capers*
    1 *tablespoon chopped olives*
    1 *teaspoon grated onion*
Chill. About 1½ cups.

Tomato Sauce
Mix well ...

    1 *cup mayonnaise*
    ¼ *cup tomato paste*
    2 *tablespoons chopped green pepper*
    2 *tablespoons chopped pimiento*
Chill. About 1½ cups.

*If some of the foods for your grill party are to travel,
keep hot ones hot and cold ones cold in a wooden
snack bucket or Scotch cooler*

Outdoor Menu

Bacon Steaks

B acon steaks are ½-in. thick slices cut from slab bacon.

Arrange on grill about 3 in. from coals . . .

>   16 *bacon steaks*

Grill over low coals about 20 min., or until evenly crisped and browned. Turn frequently.

Have handy a baster filled with water to douse flames as they flare up. 8 servings.

—Skillet-Cooked Bacon

Regular sliced bacon can be done in a skillet or flat griddle on the grill. Place bacon slices in cold heavy skillet. Cook slowly, turning frequently. Pour off fat as it accumulates. (Be careful not to pour it on coals.) Cook until evenly crisped and browned. Remove to absorbent paper on warm serving platter.

—Bacon-Tomato Sandwiches

While skillet bacon is cooking, cut 8 hamburger

buns into halves. Toast on back of grill. Brush with melted butter. Top half with tomato slices. Season with salt and pepper. Place bacon on top of tomatoes. Top with remaining bun halves and serve.

Griddlecakes

Have on deck . . .

Griddlecake batter

(You might have your first mate prepare this ahead of time and keep it in the refrigerator until you're ready to use it. Or use pancake mix and prepare batter according to directions on package.)

Heat griddle or heavy skillet on grill over low coals until drops of water dance in small beads on surface. Lightly grease griddle with. . .

Butter

Pour batter from a pitcher or large spoon into small pools about 4 in. in diameter, leaving at least 1 in. between. Turn cakes with hamburger turner when they become puffy and full of bubbles. Turn only once. Serve griddlecake stacks immediately with warm maple sirup and butter. About 18 griddlecakes.

—Griddlecake Batter

Melt and set aside . . .

2 tablespoons butter

Chef's Notes

1. Buy a side of bacon and slice it yourself, or have your meat dealer do it. Thinner slices of bacon should be done only in the skillet.

2. If you're serving a crowd, place bacon steaks back into original block form and put into bread pans. Place in oven about 15 min. at 350°F. Then separate slices and grill them. This removes much of the surplus fat and lessens danger of flare-ups.

Sift together . . .

> 1½ cups sifted flour
> 1 tablespoon sugar
> 1½ teaspoons baking powder
> ½ teaspoon salt

Make a well in center of dry ingredients.

Beat together slightly . . .

> 2 eggs
> 1⅓ cups milk

Add all at once to dry ingredients. Beat with rotary beater until well blended and smooth. Blend in melted butter. Keep batter in refrigerator until ready to use later the same day.

—Blueberry Griddlecakes

Blend 2 cups fresh blueberries into batter before baking.

—How to Flip Flapjacks

Bake griddlecakes one at a time in a heavy skillet. When cake becomes puffy and full of bubbles, it is ready to flip. Shake or loosen from bottom of skillet. Then, to toss, shake the skillet until side of cake away from you touches the edge of the skillet. Toss the far edge of the cake up into the air with a quick motion of the wrist. Catch it in the middle of the skillet when it is upside down. It will sizzle and start to brown on second side. Here practice does make perfect, so try it out before you show off in front of guests.

—Dessert Griddlecakes

Spread griddlecakes with jam or jelly. Roll up and dust with confectioners' sugar. Perfect finger fare! Or—

Top griddlecakes with sweetened crushed berries and whipped or sour cream. Or—

Generously spread hot griddlecakes with butter. Sprinkle 1 tablespoon brown sugar and chopped nuts over each cake. Roll up.

Choose outdoor menus to fit your grill space. Plan meals so that all guests are fed at the first grilling

Outdoor Menu

Grilled Canadian Style Bacon

Allow 2 or 3 slices bacon for each guest. Place on grill . . .

Canadian style bacon slices (½ in. thick)

Grill 3 in. from coals until well browned (about 5 min.). Turn and brown other sides (about 5 min.). Grill second servings later.

—Glazed Canadian Style Bacon

Baste Canadian style bacon frequently with a mixture of ½ cup orange juice and ¼ cup softened peanut butter (enough for about 8 slices meat).

Any sauce suggested for Charcoal Broiled Ham Slice (page 71) also can be used here. Or, try your favorite barbecue sauce.

—Skillet-Broiled Canadian Style Bacon

Place Canadian style bacon slices in lightly

33

greased heavy skillet. Put skillet on grill. Cook until meat is browned, turning occasionally. During last few minutes, baste with any sauce suggested for Glazed Canadian Style Bacon.

Scrambled Eggs

Mix ...

> 8 *eggs*
> ½ *cup milk or cream*
> 1 *teaspoon salt*
> ¼ *teaspoon pepper*

If you want streaks of yellow and white, mix only slightly. Mix thoroughly for a uniform yellow color. Heat a heavy skillet until hot enough to sizzle a drop of water. Melt in skillet ...

> 2 *tablespoons butter*

Pour in egg mixture. Immediately move skillet to side of grill. Cook slowly. As mixture thickens, with a spatula lift it from sides and bottom of skillet so uncooked part will flow to bottom. Cook until all of mixture is thickened but still moist. 4 to 6 servings.

—Scrambled Eggs with Bacon

Prepare Skillet Cooked Bacon (page 29), using only 3 or 4 slices of bacon, sliced thin. Crumble the crisp bacon and add to egg mixture for Scrambled Eggs. Cook the eggs in the same skillet as the bacon, using bacon drippings rather than butter.

Chef's Notes

1. *Berries and Cherries Dipped in Sugar*—Leave stems on cherries and hulls on strawberries for easy dipping in sugar—confectioners' or granulated.
2. The scrambled egg mixture can be used for a French omelet. Just cook in one mass, lifting edges to let uncooked part flow to bottom of skillet. When cooked but still moist, fold omelet in half, turn out of skillet and serve.
3. Serve plenty of butter with hot coffee cake.
4. Bakery coffee cake can be buttered and toasted on the grill.

—Scrambled Eggs with Mushrooms

Wipe caps and stems of 4 to 6 large fresh mushrooms. Slice lengthwise through caps and stems. Cook slowly about 5 min. with 2 tablespoons butter in heavy skillet. Stir gently. Add egg mixture and proceed as for Scrambled Eggs.

—Scrambled Eggs Savory

Add 2 tablespoons chopped chives and 1 teaspoon finely chopped parsley to uncooked mixture in Scrambled Eggs.

Skillet Coffee Cake

Thoroughly grease bottom of a Dutch oven or a heavy 10-in. skillet having a tight-fitting cover. Line bottom of skillet with several thicknesses of waxed paper; grease again. Set cover of skillet at edge of grill to heat thoroughly.

For Coconut Topper—Lightly mix and set aside . . .

> ¼ *cup biscuit mix (homemade or commercial)*
> ¼ *cup shredded coconut, chopped*
> 3 *tablespoons sugar*
> 2 *tablespoons grated lemon peel*
> ½ *teaspoon nutmeg*

For Coffee Cake—Blend thoroughly . . .

> 1½ *cups biscuit mix*
> ⅓ *cup sugar*

Beat until thick and piled softly . . .

> 1 *egg*

Add to mix with . . .

> ¼ *cup milk*

Beat about 100 strokes, or until batter is smooth. (Or, follow directions on package of commercial mix.) Turn into prepared skillet. Sprinkle Coconut Topper on batter. Cover skillet and place over *low* heat at edge of grill. Bake without removing cover 15 to 20 min. Cake is done if a wooden pick comes out clean when inserted in center. 6 to 8 servings.

—Jam Crested Coffee Cake

Substitute for topping of Skillet Coffee Cake a mixture of 1 cup bran or wheat flakes, 2 tablespoons brown sugar, ½ teaspoon cinnamon, ¼ teaspoon nutmeg and 3 tablespoons melted butter. Cover batter with topping. Using back of teaspoon, make small hollows at about 2-in. intervals across cake. Fill each hollow with ½ teaspoon fruit jam.

Outdoor Menu

Turkey on a Spit

Remove the spit from the grill before you build the fire so it won't heat.

Rinse well with cold water and pat dry . . .

> *1 roasting turkey, 6 to 12 lbs., ready-to-cook weight (allow ¾ lb. per person)*

Cut off neck at body. Rub cavity of turkey with . . .

> *1 to 2 teaspoons salt*

If you're ambitious you can fill the body and neck cavities with Herb Stuffing at this point. To close the body cavity, sew or skewer and lace with cord. Fasten neck skin to back with skewer. Tie wings to body and legs together. Grease skin thoroughly with . . .

> *Unsalted fat*

Insert spit lengthwise through turkey. Tie drumsticks to spit. Be sure bird is perfectly balanced. Insert thermometer into center of inside thigh muscle or (when turkey is the broad-breasted variety) into center of breast. Thermometer must not touch bone or spit.

Attach spit and place drip pan in proper position; turn on motor. Brush turkey often during roasting with . . .

Melted butter and drippings in pan

Roast until done, allowing 18-22 min. per lb. for hen turkey and 15-18 min. per lb. for tom turkey. (Thermometer should register 190°F.)

When turkey is done, remove thermometer and take bird from spit; let stand about 10 min. to become firm before carving. (Without thermometer, test for doneness by moving drumstick up and down; it will twist out of joint easily.)

Let grill wear a hood—it intensifies the cooking heat.

Herb Stuffing

Some outdoor chefs do not believe in stuffing a turkey that is to be spit roasted. However, stuffing it is an easy way to prepare main dish and side dish at the same time—that's ingenuity at work.

Mix . . .

½ cup melted butter
1½ teaspoons salt
¼ teaspoon thyme

Chef's Notes

1. Turkey lends itself easily to the out-of-door feast, so don't overlook this delicacy when you are showing off your mastery of grilling.

2. During roasting, turkey may be basted with Barbecue Sauce (see Sauce-Painted Spareribs, page 64) instead of melted butter.

3. *Stuffed Celery*—You can treat the celery with a stuffing, too. Mix equal parts of Blue and cream cheese to fill the cavities.

4. Don't forget to sprinkle lime juice over honeydew melon to give it that extra tang.

¼ *teaspoon marjoram*
¼ *teaspoon rosemary*
¼ *teaspoon pepper*

Lightly toss butter mixture with . . .

1½ *qts. soft bread cubes*
½ *cup milk*
¼ *cup chopped celery leaves*
¼ *cup chopped onion*

This makes enough stuffing to go with an 8-lb. turkey. Spoon the stuffing into the turkey body and neck cavities—do not pack it. Stuff the turkey *just before* roasting.

Wrap any extra stuffing in aluminum foil, double-folding the edges, and place on grill the last 45 min. of roasting time.

Outdoor Menu

Hot Grilled Franks
Baked Beans
Relishes: Scallions, Carrots,
Cauliflower, Olives, Pickles
Toasted Long Buns
Tart Fruit Pie   Sour Cream
Beverage

Hot Grilled Franks

Place on grill or in hot dog roaster . . .

2 frankfurters for each guest

Grill them, turning frequently, until they are lightly browned and heated through (about 10 min.). Serve with pickle relish, horseradish and mustard, chili sauce, ketchup, or a dash of all. Have hot toasted buttered buns on hand, too. Sometime try spreading mayonnaise or salad dressing on buns before toasting.

—Grilled Frankfurters with Sauce

Slit frankfurters lengthwise, almost through. Spread open. Brush with Barbecue Sauce (page 9) and grill, starting with cut side down, basting frequently.

—Bacon Wraps

Slit frankfurters almost through, lengthwise. Spread with a cheese spread; a mixture of sharp

Chef's Notes

1. *Relishes*—A variety of relishes, crisp and color-ful, are easily prepared—tempting to all who step near the laden tray. Cut carrots into sticks, break cauliflower into small flowerets; chill.

2. *Toasted Long Buns*—Cut long buns into halves. Spread cut sides with softened butter. Grill in steak broiler until slightly crisp. Serve hot with frankfurters.

3. *Tart Fruit Pie*—A dab of sour cream is a luxuri-ous addition to a one-crust fruit pie, whether it be bakery bought or kitchen brought.

grated cheese and grated onion, pickle relish or caraway seeds; or add cheese slices. Starting at one end, wrap one slice of bacon around each frankfurter; secure ends with wooden picks. Put these on grill, on skewer, or in hot dog roaster. Grill slowly, until bacon and frankfurters are lightly browned.

—Hot Dogs in Foil

Use any of the above variations for frankfurters (except Bacon Wraps). Wrap each frankfurter loosely in aluminum foil. Roast on the grill, about 6 min., turning frequently.

—Skillet Franks

If you prefer using the skillet, brown frankfurters slowly in hot butter at the side of the grill. Turn often. They'll be done in about 7 min. Have ready a Barbecue Sauce made by combining 1 small onion, finely chopped. ¼ cup finely chopped green pepper, 2 tablespoons brown sugar, 2 tablespoons prepared mustard, 2 teaspoons Worcestershire sauce, 1 teaspoon salt and ⅔ cup ketchup. Add to franks in skillet. Simmer 10 to 15 min. Serve franks with sauce.

Baked Beans

Set out a heavy skillet having a cover. Pour in . . .

2 1-lb. cans baked beans

Thoroughly mix in . . .

⅓ cup ketchup
¼ cup molasses
2 tablespoons brown sugar
2 teaspoons dry mustard
½ teaspoon monosodium glutamate
½ teaspoon salt

Top with . . .

4 bacon slices, cut into halves

Cover and cook about 30 min., or until the top is bubbling and the aroma is so tantalizing you suddenly are awfully hungry. 6 servings.

—Barbecued Baked Beans

Omit the above seasonings. Mix your favorite barbecue sauce with the beans.

—Cheese-Topped Baked Beans

You might omit the bacon slices and sprinkle top of seasoned baked beans with grated sharp Cheddar cheese.

Barbecued Bologna Roll
Kitchen-Made Scalloped Potatoes
Green Onions   Radishes
Banana Boats
Beverage

Barbecued Bologna Roll

Score with ½- to 1-in. cuts, 1 in. apart, side of . . .

4- to 6-lb. roll of bologna

Secure roll on spit or shish kebab skewer. Spread with a mixture of . . .

1½ tablespoons prepared mustard
1½ teaspoons brown sugar
1 teaspoon prepared horseradish

Attach the spit or place directly on grill about 3 in. from coals. Baste well with a mixture of . . .

1 cup chili sauce
3 tablespoons vinegar

Start motor. Grill until roll is thoroughly heated. If placed directly on grill, turn often. Remove spit or skewer; slice. About 16 servings.

—Barbecued Bologna Slices

Cut bologna roll into 1-in. slices. Double mustard mixture and spread on slices. Secure slices on shish kebab skewer to reshape roll. Grill as for Barbecued Bologna Roll.

Kitchen-Made
Scalloped Potatoes

Butter a shallow 3-qt. casserole. Heat in top of double boiler . . .

> 3½ *cups milk*

Wash, pare and slice . . .

> 8 *medium-size potatoes (about 3 lbs.)*

Shake slices in paper bag with a mixture of . . .

> 2 *tablespoons flour*
> 1 *tablespoon salt*
> ½ *teaspoon monosodium glutamate*
> ⅛ *teaspoon pepper*

Arrange potato slices in layers in casserole. Dot layers with . . .
> ¼ *cup butter*

Add hot milk until it comes barely to top of potatoes. Bake at 350°F 45 to 50 min. 8 servings.

—Cheese-Topped Potatoes

Sprinkle 1½ cups grated Cheddar cheese between layers and on top of potatoes.

—Oranges and Sweets

Thinly slice 1 orange and arrange on bottom of

Chef's Notes

1. The bologna roll might be roasted on the lowest position of the spit.

2. For variety, baste the bologna roll with your favorite barbecue sauce.

3. For "super" seasoning, add ½ cup chopped onion to layers of Kitchen-Made Scalloped Potatoes.

buttered casserole. Sprinkle with 2 tablespoons brown sugar. Slice 8 cooked or canned medium-size sweet potatoes into 1½-in. rounds and place on orange slices. Stud with whole cloves. Cover and bake at 350°F about 20 min. Meanwhile, mix in a skillet 1½ cups brown sugar and ⅓ cup orange juice; bring to boiling and boil 5 min. Stir in ¼ cup butter and pour over baked sweet potatoes and oranges.

Banana Boats

Place on flattest side . . .

Green-tipped or all-yellow bananas,
1 for each guest

Pull back part of upper section of banana peel (do not pull off). Cut a trench the full length of the banana. (You can eat the cut-out banana.) Poke into trench, along length of banana . . .

1 cut-up marshmallow

Along side of marshmallow place . . .

Small milk chocolate pieces

Pull banana peel back into place over filling. Place banana on grill, flat side down. Roast until skin is black. Pull skin back as you eat banana.

Desserts that carry their own dishes—melons, bananas—lighten dishwashing details

Outdoor Menu

Kebabs
Salted Nuts   Buttered Rice
Cheese-Stuffed Celery
Buttered Toasted Buns (14)
Camp Caramel Apples
Beverage

Kebabs

KEBABS are skewer arrangements of morsels of varied but friendly foods. Two, three or even four pieces of each kind of food are grilled together on a metal shish kebab skewer. Juices and aromas team up to create masterpieces of magic new flavors.

Possibilities for combinations of food are endless, limited only by imagination and appetite. Some outdoor chefs plan assortments of kebab material—their "come and get it," means that guests choose, skewer and grill their own alternating array of tempting bits. Other chefs prefer to do their own planning and grilling. And, of course, there can be some combination of the two methods.

Piping-hot kebabs may be pushed off the skewers right onto waiting plates or toasted split buns. Then just pass the ketchup, barbecue sauce or what-have-you.

Measure your kebabs with the yardstick of imagination but use a few practical tricks to assure the kebab supreme. . . .

Cut meat, large vegetables and fruits into 1- to 1½-in. pieces. Small fruits and vegetables may be left whole. Plan on at least one skewer and ¼ lb. lean, boneless meat per guest and for yourself. More meat may be needed when you combine it with fewer contrasting foods. Amounts of fruits and vegetables depend on size and kind used. If some foods need longer cooking periods, they can be impaled on separate skewers, grilled and combined for eating—or they can be precooked before grilling. Or, those needing considerably less time may be added to skewers during the last few minutes of grilling.

Marinating meats and vegetables (allowing pieces to stand in seasoned liquid, usually an oil and vinegar or lemon juice mixture, to improve flavor) often is desirable. Refrigerate in marinade for an hour or longer, turning pieces from time to time if they're not covered with liquid. Use French dressing, sauces given elsewhere in this book, or work out your own fa-

47

vorite combination of flavors.

Some of the many flavors which may be incorporated in the marinade include soy, Worcestershire and tabasco sauces, wine and tarragon vinegars, fruit juices, brown sugar, ginger, mint, garlic, onion, freshly ground pepper, bay leaves, thyme, oregano, or other spices and herbs of your choice. Starred (*) foods in the list of suggested combinations for kebabs are improved by marinating.

The same marinade may be used for basting (to keep kebabs moist) during grilling; or use it as a basting agent only. Melted butter is a simple but de luxe baster. Bacon, too, does a top job of basting. Cut slices into squares and pin between other pieces of food; leave it in strips and impale gradually, zigzag fashion, along the skewer, alternating it with the other foods; or wrap cut slices around individual pieces of food.

Place kebab morsels rather closely together if you like the food rare; separate them slightly for a well-done dinner.

Grill kebabs on greased grill about 3 in. from the bed of coals, turning them almost constantly. Or arrange several in your greased steak or hamburger broiler. Another plan is to brown the kebab, then wrap in aluminum foil and continue grilling until tender. (Slices of uncooked potato or onion cook beautifully this way.) Grilling periods range from 5 to 20 min., or until kebabs are tender and that luscious brown color you love to see.

Keep delicious juices in your kebabs—season the fragrant morsels to taste after they're slipped off the skewer.

No more directions—the world of kebabs is yours for the exploring. *Starting Points* (a few suggestions for combinations of food) . . .

Beef (loin, top round or round) *Sirloin steak, large fresh mushroom caps. . . . *Sirloin, cooked small onion, small unpeeled tomatoes, green pepper squares. . . . *Steak, bacon. . . . *Beef, *lamb, *precooked ham. . . . Hamburger or meat loaf mixture (with garlic), shaped in balls to fit rolls, small cooked onions. . . . *Beef (or lamb), apple or pineapple chunks, cooked onions, bacon. . . . Calf's liver, bacon, small cooked onions. . . . Bacon, sweetbreads, mushroom caps.

Lamb (loin, leg or shoulder) *Lamb, bacon, mushroom caps. . . . *Lamb, bacon, pineapple and cucumber pickle chunks. . . . *Lamb kidneys, *beef, small cooked onions, mushroom caps. . . . Ground lamb, bacon, mushroom caps, apples, small cooked onions. . . . *Lamb, green pepper slices, small tomatoes, bacon.

Pork (shoulder, loin—must be precooked before grilling to assure complete doneness) *Pork, apples. . . . Sausage balls (or links), apple quarters, cooked onions. . . . Thinly sliced ham rolled around pineapple chunks or Swiss cheese cubes.

Sausage and Ready-to-Serve Meats (baste well) Frankfurters, cheese cubes wrapped in bacon. . . . Franks, sweet pickles, bacon, small cooked onions. . . . Franks spread with prepared mustard, apple chunks, bacon. . . . Split franks enclosing cheese, wrapped in bacon. . . . Canned luncheon meat or bologna, olives, green pepper slices, bacon. . . . Bologna chunks brushed with prepared mustard, pineapple and banana chunks.

Poultry °Chicken livers, mushroom caps, bacon. . . . °Chunks of cooked turkey or chicken, precooked ham, tiny red tomatoes.

Fish and Shell Fish °Fish fillet cubes, small cooked potatoes, bacon, unpeeled tomato wedges. . . . °Peeled and deveined shrimp, °scallops, bacon. . . .°Peeled and deveined shrimp, °pineapple chunks. . . . Oysters wrapped in bacon.

Vegetables. See page 92.

Appetizers. String up small skewers with any of the following: Large stuffed olives, cubes of pineapple or cheese wrapped in bacon; marinated chicken livers; cocktail or Vienna sausages; tiny meat balls; pickled onions.

Chef's Notes

1. *Salted Nuts*—Melt 1 tablespoon butter in heavy skillet. Add 1 cup nuts. Heat, stirring constantly, until nuts are golden brown. Drain on absorbent paper. Sprinkle with salt.

2. *Cheese-Stuffed Celery*—Line up various prepared cheese spreads. Celery then can be stuffed with your guests' favorite cheese.

3. *Buttered Rice*—The popular dish to serve with Kebabs is rice. Try heating cooked rice, which should be placed in a skillet, in lots and lots of butter.

Camp Caramel Apples

For each diner, wash . . .

1 medium-size or small tart cooking apple

Spear through stem end on a shish kebab skewer. Lay apple on lightly greased grill or hold over coals. Roast, turning occasionally, until skin breaks and may be easily pulled off. Peel. Dip in a bowl of . . .

Melted butter

Immediately dip and twirl, covering apple completely, in a deep bowl of . . .

Brown sugar

Hold apple over grill, turning slowly and constantly, until it is covered with a rich caramel coating.

—Nut-Tipped Apples

As soon as sugar is melted on apple, quickly dip top in finely chopped nuts.

—Toasty Coconut Apples

Dip peeled apples in sweetened condensed milk. Coat with finely chopped shredded coconut; toast.

Outdoor Menu

Grilled Lobster
Lettuce   Thousand Island Dressing (63)
Ripe Olives
Grilled French Bread
Honeydew Quarters with Raspberries
Beverage

Grilled Lobster

Purchase for each guest (being sure to include yourself) . . .

1 live lobster (about 1½ lbs. each)

Live lobsters may be killed and dressed for cooking at the market. If prepared at home, place the lobster on a cutting board with back or smooth shell up. Hold a towel firmly over the head and claws. Kill by quickly inserting the point of a sharp heavy knife into the center of the small cross showing on the back of the head.

Without removing knife, quickly bear down heavily, cutting through entire length of the body and tail. Split the halves apart and remove the stomach, a small sac which lies in the head, and the spongy lungs which lie between meat and shell. Also remove the dark intestinal line running through the center of the body. Crack large claws with a nut cracker or mallet.
Brush meat with . . .

Lemon Butter Sauce (page 56)

Place shell side down on grill about 5 in. from

coals Grill about 20 min., or until shell is browned. Baste frequently with butter sauce.

Serve in shell with rest of Lemon Butter Sauce. Here is one place where picnic forks are definitely acceptable.

—Boiled Lobster

Boiled lobster may be done on your grill, too—if you have a large kettle.

Plunge live lobster head first in rapidly boiling salt water (1 tablespoon per quart of water). Cover and boil about 8 min. (Lobster will turn pink.) Remove with tongs. Slit underside and remove stomach, lungs and vein. Serve lobster with Lemon Butter Sauce (page 56).

Grilled French Bread

Make diagonal cuts from ½ to ¾ in. apart almost through . . .

1 loaf French bread

Spread one of the *Butters* described below on top of bread and between slices. Place loaf on aluminum foil large enough to cover bread completely. Wrap loosely all around loaf, closing ends with a double fold.

Place on grill about 10 min., or until heated entirely through. Turn frequently for even heating. Serve piping hot, letting each guest break off his own portion.

Garlic Butter—Crush 1 clove garlic with ¼ teaspoon salt to form a smooth paste. Blend with ½ cup softened butter.

Chef's Notes

1. A steady hand and a firm grip on the chef's knife will keep the situation under control for you and your live lobster.

2. Lettuce may be served in various ways: slices, wedges, chunks—any way you choose. Tomato chunks and cucumber slices are gay additions.

3. *Quarters of Honeydew*—Fresh ripe raspberries piled high in honeydew melon is the dessert for this seafood lover's meal. Or you might prefer blueberries or strawberries. Point up melon flavor with lime juice. Set out the shaker of confectioners sugar.

Blue Cheese Butter—Blend to spreading consistency ½ cup softened butter and 1 oz. Roquefort or Blue cheese, crumbled.

Poppy Seed Butter—Blend ½ cup softened butter with ¼ cup poppy seeds.

Sharp Butter—Blend ½ cup softened butter with ½ cup grated sharp Cheddar cheese, 2 tablespoons finely chopped onion, 1 tablespoon lemon juice and a drop of tabasco sauce.

Herb Butter—Blend ½ cup softened butter with ½ teaspoon dried tarragon and 2 tablespoons chopped chives.

—Cheese French Bread

Spread bread slices with softened butter and mustard. Place a slice of Cheddar cheese and an

onion slice in each slit. Grill as for Grilled French
Bread.

—Toasted French Bread

Hunks of French bread may be toasted on the
grill or on a stick or fork over low coals. Spread
with one of the *Butters* before and after toasting.
Serve immediately.

—French Rolls

French rolls also can be grilled like French
bread. For a flavor treat place slices of smoked
cheese in buttered bread slits.

Outdoor Menu

Melon Chunks on Picks
Rock-Lobster Tails   Lemon Butter Sauce
Lettuce Chef's Style   Flavorful Asparagus
Tomato Slices   Olives   Brown-Only Rolls
Lemon Sherbet   Beverage

Rock-Lobster Tails

Thaw . . .

*1 12-oz. fresh-frozen rock-lobster tail for
each person*

Snip through and remove thin shell on underside; remove vein. Holding tail in both hands,
bend it towards shell side to crack, or insert a
skewer lengthwise through meat. This keeps tail
flat. (If you can buy fresh rock-lobster tails, your
fish dealer may do this for you.)

Place tails shell-side down on grill about 4 in.
or more from coals; brush with . . .

Lemon Butter Sauce

Grill about 10 min., or until shell is charred,
brushing with sauce occasionally. Be sure not to
let the fire get too hot. Turn tails with tongs and
continue grilling about 6 min., or until meat is
completely white and opaque. Serve with remaining butter sauce and lemon wedges or lots
of melted butter.

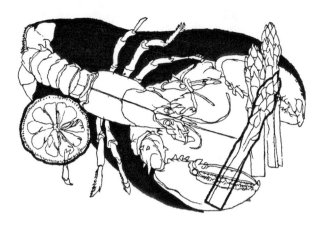

Lemon Butter Sauce

Heat together in a small pan . . .

> 1 *cup butter*
> 2 *tablespoons lemon juice*
> ¼ *teaspoon salt*
> ¼ *teaspoon paprika*
> ⅛ *teaspoon pepper*

This will make plenty for basting and serving.

Add, if you wish . . .

> ¼ *cup chopped parsley*

About 1 cup sauce.

Brown-Only Rolls

Have a skillet handy, ready for browning these rolls. Grease the bottom of skillet.

Place in skillet . . .

> *Brown-only rolls*

Chef's Notes

1. Cooked asparagus spears (fresh, frozen or canned) can share the same sauce with the rock-lobster tails.

2. *Melon Chunks on Picks*—Insert wooden picks in chunks of watermelon, honeydew melon or cantaloupe; chill. Use the scooped-out melon shell as a server. Add a few bing cherries with stems on.

3. *Lettuce Chef's Style*—As chef, you dictate the style of serving the lettuce and choose a dressing for it.

4. *Lemon Sherbet*—Keep sherbet as cold as you got it from the grocer by wrapping it in newspapers and dry ice.

Brush with melted butter. Cover tightly and set skillet on the grill—just to the side. Allow about 8 min. for browning. During this time, turn rolls occasionally.

They'll turn out hot and wonderful while you're chef-working with the Rock-Lobster Tails.

Aluminum foil, wrapped loosely all around the rolls, substitutes easily for a skillet. Be sure to double-fold the edges. Brush rolls with butter before wrapping. Remember to turn package once to brown second side.

Make your own variations by sprinkling one of these over the top of butter-brushed rolls . . .

> *Poppy or caraway seeds*
> *Grated cheese*
> *Brown sugar*
> *Orange or pineapple juice*

Be sure to plan on enough quick hot rolls.

Outdoor Menu

Duckling on a Spit
Grilled Tomatoes   Baked Potatoes
Cucumbers in Sour Cream
Buttered Rolls
Fresh Peaches 'n' Lime Sherbet
Beverage

Duckling on a Spit

To prevent its heating, remove spit from grill before building fire.

Clean, rinse and dry with absorbent paper . . .

1 duckling, 5 lbs., ready-to-cook weight

Rub cavity with about . . .

1½ teaspoons salt

Wash, cut in half, core and pare . . .

1 large, tart apple

Wash, core and pare . . .

1 medium-size tart apple

Place apple halves in cavity of duckling. Insert whole apple in neck opening; fasten neck skin to back with skewers. Insert spit lengthwise through bird. Tie drumsticks to spit by looping cord over tip ends and around spit. Repeat with wings. Be sure duckling is well balanced. Attach spit; place drip pan in position. Start motor and grill about 1½ hrs. When using a hand-pro-

58

pelled-type spit, turn bird frequently while roasting. Baste often with . . .

> *2 cups orange juice*
> *1 teaspoon grated orange peel*

When duckling is done, carve; put pieces in orange juice-dripping mixture. Place pan over coals several minutes to glaze meat with juice. 4 servings.

Baked Potatoes in Foil

Wash, scrub and wipe dry . . .

> *4 baking potatoes*

Rub fat over entire surface of potatoes and wrap each loosely in aluminum foil. Seal open ends with a double fold. Place on grill and bake about 1 hr., or until tender. Turn several times for even baking. Loosen foil and make a slit in top of potato to see if it is done. Cut cross in top of potato and pinch open. Place in center of each . . .

> *1 tablespoon butter*
> *Sprinkle of salt*
> *Sprinkle of paprika*

Skins and all are edible when potatoes are baked this way. 4 servings.

—Cheese Baked Potatoes

Bake potatoes and when tender, cut cross in top and pinch open. Scoop out spoonful of potato. Stuff in a cube of cheese, 1 tablespoon butter, ¼

Chef's Notes

1. When cooking in foil, remember to make a loose package and don't puncture the foil. Be sure to seal ends with a double fold.

2. *Cucumbers in Sour Cream*—Slice cucumbers into sour cream mixed with a little vinegar, a little sugar, and salt and pepper to taste.

3. *Grilled Tomatoes*—Tomatoes, cut into halves, brushed with melted butter and seasoned, can be put on the grill during the last three minutes when you are dishing up the rest of the meal.

4. *Fresh Peaches 'n' Lime Sherbet*—Refreshing dessert partners, and as handy as your nearest grocer.

teaspoon salt and cover with the spoonful of potato. Rewrap in foil. Bake about 10 min. more, or until cheese is melted. Or, sprinkle a tablespoon of Parmesan cheese on potato when adding butter.

—Herb Baked Potatoes

Chopped parsley or chives added to butter, chilled and rolled into balls, makes an herb butter par excellence.

Cut a cross in top of baked potato and pinch open. Top with herb butter ball and a sprinkle of paprika.

—Baked Sweets

Wrap scrubbed sweet potatoes loosely in aluminum foil. Seal open ends with a double fold. Bake about 45 min. Make a slit in top of each. Place 1 teaspoon each of brown sugar and butter in center.

Outdoor Menu

Frogs' Legs Feast

Wash and dry . . .

>   *2 pairs large skinned frogs' legs, or 4 pairs*
>   *small skinned frogs' legs for each*
>   *serving*

(If you prepare them yourself, cut off hind legs
from body of frog. Remove feet. Peel skin from
leg starting at the thigh.)

Marinate about 30 min. in . . .

>   *Lemon Butter Sauce (page 56. Use ¼*
>   *cup lemon juice.)*

Turn several times. Drain, reserving marinade.
Place frogs' legs in greased steak broiler and grill
about 3 in. from coals. Grill about 5 min. on each
side, or until tender. Baste with marinade every
few minutes. Serve with hot Lemon Butter
Sauce.

—Fried Frogs' Legs

Soak frogs' legs in salt water (1 tablespoon per 2
quarts water) 15 min.; drain. Coat with a mix-

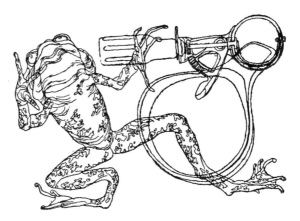

ture of flour, salt, monosodium glutamate and pepper. Heat butter in skillet. Split a clove of garlic and cook in butter about 4 min. Remove garlic and brown frogs' legs in the butter until golden brown (about 20 min.). Drain and serve with Lemon Butter Sauce (page 56).

—Frogs' Legs aux Fines Herbes

Another gala feast you will have when you fry frogs' legs and serve them with Dressing aux Fines Herbes. To make the dressing, blend 1 tablespoon each of chopped chervil, chives, tarragon and parsley into 1 cup mayonnaise.

Prepare Fried Frogs' Legs. Serve with lemon wedge and Dressing aux Fines Herbes.

Combination Soup

Combine in heavy kettle or warming pot the contents of . . .

1 10½-oz. can condensed green pea soup
1 10½-oz. can condensed cream of
    mushroom soup

Chef's Notes

1. Never heat canned foods in unopened cans. Serious injuries may result from exploding cans.

2. *Grilled Cornbread*—Cut cornbread squares into halves. Spread with softened butter and sprinkle with paprika. Place in steak broiler. Toast both sides a golden brown. Serve hot with more butter.

3. Dip frogs' legs in cream before coating with seasoned flour, then fry to a rich brown.

Blend in (use empty can to measure) . . .

   2 cans milk

Cook over low coals just to boiling (do not boil). Stir occasionally. Cover and keep soup hot on side of grill until ready to serve. 6 servings.

Thousand Island Dressing

Combine . . .

   1 cup mayonnaise
   ¼ cup chili sauce
   2 tablespoons chopped green pepper
   2 tablespoons chopped stuffed olives
   1 tablespoon chopped chives
   1 diced hard-cooked egg
   ½ teaspoon paprika

Blend in . . .

   ¼ cup whipping cream, whipped

Serve over thick wedges of lettuce. About 2 cups.

Outdoor Menu
Sauce-Painted Spareribs
Cole Slaw   Roast Corn (10)
Relishes   Cheese French Rolls (53)
Freezer Ice Cream (14)
Beverage

Sauce-Painted Spareribs

Cut into he-man-size portions . . .

4 lbs. spareribs

Partially roast meat (about 30 min.) in kitchen oven at 350°F. Then, place meaty side down on grill. Slowly grill about 3 in. from hot coals. Turn about every 5 min., brushing with Barbecue Sauce. Grill until meat is a deep brown and crisp (about 25 min.). 8 servings.

Barbecue Sauce—You can prepare this a day or two ahead and store in refrigerator. Then heat on the grill just before using. Like wine, this sauce improves with age.

Combine in saucepan . . .

1 cup ketchup
¼ cup lemon juice
2 tablespoons brown sugar
1 tablespoon soy sauce
1 tablespoon prepared horseradish
    mustard

64

1 tablespoon grated onion
1½ teaspoons salt
½ teaspoon monosodium glutamate
½ teaspoon pepper
¼ teaspoon oregano, marjoram or thyme
¼ teaspoon tabasco sauce
¼ teaspoon cayenne pepper
1 clove garlic

Simmer over low heat at least 10 min. Remove garlic. Use immediately or store.

—Barbecued Ribs, Hawaiian

Pour over ribs a mixture of ½ cup soy sauce, ¼ cup cornstarch and 3 tablespoons chopped preserved or candied ginger. Let stand about 30 min., turning frequently. Roast and grill as usual, brushing with a mixture of ¾ cup sugar, ½ cup pineapple juice and 3 tablespoons vinegar.

Chef's Notes

1. Precooking the spareribs in the kitchen shortens cooking time on the grill. Also, it insures thorough cooking of the meat.

2. Keep baster handy for flare-ups.

3. Ribs are finger food—so have plenty of paper napkins handy.

4. For a dramatic Cole Slaw, cut out the center and almost to edge of a firm cabbage head. Shred the interior for the salad mixture. Spoon completed salad into this shell and serve.

Cole Slaw

Blend . . .

> ½ *cup sour cream*
> 2 *tablespoons sugar*
> 2 *tablespoons vinegar*
> 1 *teaspoon salt*
> ¼ *teaspoon pepper*

Pour over and toss with . . .

> 4 *cups shredded cabbage*
> ½ *cup chopped onion*
> 2 *teaspoons celery seed*

Chill before serving. Sprinkle with . . .

> *Paprika*

4 servings.

—Sunshine Slaw

Toss ½ cup shredded carrot and ½ cup chopped green pepper with Cole Slaw.

—Pineapple-Cabbage Salad

Add 2 cups well-drained crushed pineapple and 1 cup chopped nuts. to Cole Slaw. Omit onion and celery seed.

Outdoor Menu

Hot Plate Lamb Chops
Baked Squash
Herb Buttered Green Beans
Brown-Only Rolls (56)
Green and Ripe Olives
Chilled Fruits
Beverage

Hot Plate Lamb Chops

Mix and set aside . . .

>   2 *teaspoons salt*
>   1 *teaspoon monosodium glutamate*
>   ⅛ *teaspoon freshly ground pepper*

Trim most of fat from . . .

>   4 *lamb chops, such as loin, rib, arm*
>   *or blade, cut 1 to 1½ in. thick*

Rub each side of meat with cut side of . . .

>   ½ *clove garlic*

Lightly grease grill with . . .

>   *Cooking oil*

Place chops on grill about 4 in. from coals. Grill about 8 min., or until meat is browned. Turn and season with half of seasoning mixture. Grill second side about 8 min., or until done. To test

67

doneness, slit meat near bone and note color of meat. Season other side and serve immediately on hot plates. 4 servings.

—Barbecued Lamb Chops

Omit garlic and other seasonings. During grilling brush frequently with Special Barbecue Sauce for Lamb.

—Curried Lamb Chops

Omit garlic and other seasonings. Brush chops with Curry Sauce during grilling. Why not serve with them some of the condiments usually served with Indian curry, such as fresh coconut, chopped peanuts, avocado slices, chopped whites and sieved yolks of hard-cooked eggs, chopped green pepper, scallions, chives, tomato quarters and, of course, chutney—?

Chef's Notes

1. Here is a menu for a Sunday morning brunch.

2. *Herb Buttered Green Beans* (page 57)—Mash 1 teaspoon dill seed in a wooden bowl. Mix with 2 tablespoons melted butter. Let this stand while cooking green beans. Then pour dill butter over beans and serve. See Vegetable Cookery for the Grill, page 93, for cooking beans.

3. *Chilled Fruits*—Serve fruits such as orange and grapefruit sections, grapes, fresh pineapple spears, cherries and berries lightly sprinkled with confectioners' sugar.

Special Barbecue Sauce for Lamb

Combine . . .

> ½ *cup water*
> ¼ *cup lemon juice*
> 12 *fresh mint leaves, crushed*
> 2 *cloves garlic, split*
> 2 *tablespoons finely chopped onion*
> 1 *teaspoon rosemary*

Let stand overnight. Remove garlic and mint leaves. Use sauce for basting lamb chops.

A rule-of-thumb for all chefs—serve hot foods really hot, and cold foods icy cold

Curry Sauce

Mix . . .

> ¾ *cup salad oil*
> 3 *tablespoons lemon juice*
> 2 *tablespoons sugar*
> 1 *small onion, chopped*
> 1 *clove garlic, split*
> 2 *teaspoons curry powder*
> 1½ *teaspoons salt*
> ½ *teaspoon monosodium glutamate*
> ½ *teaspoon freshly ground pepper*

Cook slowly 10 min. Remove garlic. Use sauce
for basting lamb chops.

Baked Squash

Split into halves . . .

> 1 *acorn squash for each pair of guests*

Remove seed sections. Wrap each half loosely in
heavy aluminum foil. Double fold open edges to
seal. Place squash on grill, cut-side down. Grill
about 30 min., or until inside of squash is tender.

Put in cavity of each squash half . . .

> 1 *tablespoon molasses*
> 1 *tablespoon butter*
> 2 *teaspoons brown sugar*

Be sure to start this soon enough so that it can be
served when the meat is done.

Charcoal Broiled Ham Slice   Fried Eggs
Grilled Pineapple Slices
Toasted Sweet Rolls
Beverage

Charcoal Broiled Ham Slice

Purchase for every 2 or 3 guests . . .

1 ham slice (½ in. thick)

Grill 3 in. from coals, basting with a mixture of . . .

½ cup sour cream
1½ tablespoons prepared horseradish
    mustard

Turn and baste often to keep ham moist. Grill until ham is tender (about 10 min.).

—Grilled Ham Slice with Barbecue Sauce

Combine ¼ cup ketchup, ¼ cup vinegar, ¼ cup water, ½ teaspoon celery seed and ½ teaspoon dry mustard. Use for basting Charcoal Broiled Ham Slice.

—Grilled Ham with Pineapple Sauce

Grill ham as in Charcoal Broiled Ham Slice, basting with a mixture of ¾ cup pineapple juice, ½ cup brown sugar, ¼ cup vinegar and 2½ teaspoons dry mustard.

—Skillet-Broiled Ham Slice

Place ham slice in heavy skillet. Put skillet on grill. Turn meat occasionally. Cook until meat is tender (about 15 min.). Turn and baste frequently with any of the sauces suggested for Grilled Ham.

—Breakfast Ham Slice

Grill ham as directed in Charcoal Broiled Ham Slice, but omit basting with cream mixture. Instead, brush often with pineapple juice.

Grilled Pineapple Slices

Drain . . .

> *Canned pineapple slices (1 or 2 for each guest)*

Brush with . . .

> *Melted butter*

Dip in . . .

> *Brown sugar*

Grill until golden brown, turning once. Pineap-

Chef's Notes

1. Try grilling grapefruit or green-tipped bananas in their skins. Turn bananas frequently on grill until skins are black; centers will be soft. Place grapefruit halves on grill, cut-side up. Sprinkle with brown sugar. Grill until brown sugar is melted.

2. *Toasted Sweet Rolls*—Cut thick sweet rolls into halves. Brush cut side with melted butter. Place halves on grill, cut-side down. Brush bottom of thin rolls with butter and place buttered-side down on grill. Toast lightly.

3. This is a versatile sort of menu. Serve it for breakfast, brunch, lunch or supper. When it is a supper menu, Baked Sweets (page 60) are a welcome addition.

ple slices also are delicious when grilled without the sugar coating.

Peach halves can be grilled in the same way.

—Grilled Fresh Pineapple

Cut fresh pineapple lengthwise into ½-in. slices; pare and core. Generously spread slices with softened butter and drizzle 1 to 2 tablespoons honey over each slice. Grill as for canned pineapple.

Fried Eggs

Allow 2 eggs for each guest.

Heat a large heavy skillet just hot enough to sizzle a drop of water. Melt in it . . .

2 tablespoons butter

Break into a saucer . . .
  1 *egg*

Slip egg into skillet. Repeat with remaining eggs.
Move skillet to edge of grill immediately. Cook
slowly 3 to 4 min., basting with butter. Or, cover
skillet during cooking. For those who prefer
their fried eggs hard, break the yolks, turn the
eggs and cook another 1 or 2 min.

—Eggs Surprise

Cook 2 medium-size onions, thinly sliced, in
skillet with ¼ cup butter. Slip eggs over onions.
Season. Sprinkle with 2 teaspoons dry bread
crumbs for each egg. Cover skillet and cook
slowly until eggs are firm. Top each egg with 1
tablespoon grated cheese. Cook until cheese
melts.

Outdoor Menu

Honeydew Melon Halves
Trout in Bacon Wrap
Country Fried Potatoes
Tomato Hunks
Beverage

Trout in Bacon Wrap

Serve one small trout (about 10 oz.) for each guest.

Season each cleaned and scaled trout with a mixture of . . .

> 1 *teaspoon salt*
> ½ *teaspoon monosodium glutamate*
> ¼ *teaspoon paprika*
> ⅛ *teaspoon pepper*

Wrap each fish completely in . . .

> 2 or 3 *bacon slices*

Fasten with small skewers or wooden picks. Place fish in basket steak broiler. Grill 3 in. from coals, turning once, until bacon is very crisp (about 7 min.). Trout will then be cooked. Serve with . . .

> *Lemon Butter Sauce (page 56)*

Serve trout on warm plates.

—Grilled Trout

Prepare trout for grilling as in Trout in Bacon Wrap, but omit bacon slices. Baste trout frequently with Lemon Butter Sauce during grilling. Serve on a heated platter with lemon slices and the remaining butter sauce.

With or without the bacon wrap, grilled trout is certain to win a hearty vote of approval.

—Panfried Trout

Roll trout in mixture of flour and seasonings. Melt butter in heavy skillet. Add trout and fry until golden brown (15 to 20 min.). Turn frequently. Serve on a heated platter. For dinner, serve the trout with a Quick Fish Sauce (page 27-28).

Furnish each guest with his own individual serving cup of a Quick Fish Sauce. Use paper cups for easy disposal.

Country Fried Potatoes

Place flat in cold skillet . . .

> 6 *slices bacon*

Cook slowly at side of grill, turning frequently. When bacon is evenly browned and crisped, remove from skillet and set aside. Leave in skillet about . . .

> ¼ *cup bacon drippings*

Chef's Notes

1. Add a perfect touch to grilled fish with an appetizing garnish such as lemon wedges, finely chopped hard-cooked eggs, tomato wedges, chopped parsley or chives, or a Quick Fish Sauce (page 27-28).

2. Game fish usually is served with head and tail on.

3. Try a bit of pimiento or chopped chives in Country Fried Potatoes.

4. Just a simple addition of dessert will turn this hearty breakfast into a complete dinner.

Add . . .

> 6 or 7 peeled and sliced, cold cooked
> potatoes (see How to Cook Potatoes,
> page 27)

Sprinkle with a mixture of . . .

> ¾ teaspoon salt
> ½ teaspoon paprika
> ¼ teaspoon monosodium glutamate
> ⅛ teaspoon pepper

Brown potatoes well, turning only occasionally.
Crumble bacon and add shortly before serving.
6 or 7 servings.

—Lyonnaise Potatoes

Use ¼ cup bacon drippings or butter for frying. Peel 1 medium-size onion and chop fine. Cook in fat about 5 min. If you like garlic, split one clove and cook with half an onion, chopped; remove garlic. Add cooked potatoes to skillet, season and brown as in Country Fried Potatoes. Sprinkle with chopped parsley.

—Fried Sweets

Substitute cooked sweet potatoes for white. Peel and slice evenly, all crosswise or all lengthwise, not too thin. Cook with bacon fat as in Country Fried Potatoes or use ¼ cup butter. Combine 1 tablespoon brown sugar with seasonings. Turn slices carefully to prevent breaking.

Outdoor Menu

Liver Steak

Wipe with damp cloth and cut into serving-size pieces . . .

> 1 *lb. calf's or beef liver, ½ in. thick*

Brush with . . .

> *Melted butter*

Place on greased grill or in greased steak broiler 3 in. from coals. Turn occasionally. Grill until outside is slightly charred but the inside is still pink and juicy (about 10 min.). Sprinkle both sides with a mixture of . . .

> 1 *teaspoon salt*
> ¼ *teaspoon pepper*

4 servings.

—Skillet Liver Steaks

Combine seasonings with ⅓ cup flour and use it to coat liver slices. Heat 2 tablespoons butter in heavy skillet. Brown liver on both sides.

Onion Rings

Wash and peel . . .

> *1 or 2 onions for each guest*

Slice ¼ in. thick and separate slices into rings. Heat in heavy skillet over hot coals . . .

> *2 to 4 tablespoons butter*

Cook onions in skillet until tender and golden, turning often. Serve with soy or meat sauce.

Roast Carrots

Cook carrots for this well in advance. For about 8 to 10 carrots , melt in heavy skillet . . .

> *1 or 2 tablespoons butter*

Toss . . .

> *Cooked carrots, whole, slices or strips*

Chef's Notes

1. Cook liver in minimum time. Over-cooking makes it dry and less tender.
2. Whole calf's liver can be spit roasted if tied in compact form. Brush with melted butter during roasting. Or wrap bacon slices around liver and fasten with skewers.
3. *Canned Shoestring Potatoes*—Heat quickly and easily in a heavy covered skillet over hot coals. Shake the skillet frequently as you would a corn popper.
4. Let your friends bring the Brownies and the Mint Ice Cream.

in a mixture of . . .

> 1 *cup flour*
> 1 *teaspoon salt*
> ½ *teaspoon monosodium glutamate*
> ⅛ *teaspoon pepper*
> *Pinch of dried tarragon*

Heat carrots in hot butter until handsomely browned, turning frequently. This will take about 10 min.

Whole cooked carrots also can be dipped in butter and rolled in crushed corn flakes. Then place them in steak broiler and grill over hot coals until browned on both sides.

Glazed carrots can be done on the grill by adding 1 or 2 tablespoons sugar to melted butter in a skillet. Stir until sugar is dissolved before adding uncoated, cooked whole carrots or cooked carrot strips. Roll carrots in skillet until evenly glazed.

Watch your timing so all dishes reach the table simultaneously

Outdoor Menu

Citrus Pickups
Roasted Leg of Lamb
Gold Rush Fries
Plum Tomatoes—Cucumber Sticks
Bread 'n' Butter Pickles
Brown-Only Rolls (56) with Mint Butter
Freezer Ice Cream (14)
with Hot Fudge Sauce
Beverage

Roast
Leg of Lamb

Remove spit from hooded grill before building fire so spit will not heat. Cut slits in . . .

> *6-lb. boned and rolled leg of lamb roast*

Stick into slits . . .

> *Slivers of garlic or pieces of fresh mint leaves*

Insert spit; be sure roast is evenly balanced. Insert thermometer. Put drip pan in place; start motor. Baste with . . .

> *Special Barbecue Sauce for Lamb (page 69)*

Roast about 25 min. per lb. for medium done

Chef's Notes

1. *Citrus Pickups*—Orange and grapefruit wedges, chilled to cool tartness, are the "pickups" of this finger appetizer.
2. Plum or cherry tomatoes, so little and red, make a tempting mouthful.
3. *Mint Butter*—Finely cut ½ cup fresh mint leaves and cream with ½ cup softened butter. Beat in 2 tablespoons lemon juice until creamy. Spread on rolls.
4. *Hot Fudge Sauce*—While eating, heat fudge sauce, your own or store-bought, on the side of the grill. Then it will be hot when ice cream time comes.

(170°F); 30 min. per lb. for well done (180°F). Carve and serve hot. 8 to 10 servings.

Boned and rolled lamb shoulder may be used.

—Roasted Loin of Lamb

Cut between each rib three-fourths through a 4-lb. loin of lamb roast. Secure meat lengthwise on spit, directly through center of loin. Place on grill 6 in. from coals. Frequently turn and baste with Special Barbecue Sauce for Lamb (page 69). Roast about 1 hr. When done, carve meat into individual "roasts."

Gold Rush Fries

Wash and pare . . .

> 6 to 8 *medium-size (6 cups sliced)*
> *potatoes*

Cut crosswise into extra-thin slices. Heat in

heavy skillet having a cover (or use aluminum foil) . . .

⅓ *cup butter*

Add potato slices. Sprinkle with a mixture of . . .

1¼ *teaspoons salt*
¼ *teaspoon monosodium glutamate*
⅛ *teaspoon pepper*

Cover and place on grill. Cook slowly without stirring 10 to 15 min., or until underside is golden brown and crispy. Turn potatoes with hamburger turner. Leave pan uncovered and continue slow cooking 15 to 20 min. longer, or until other side is browned and potatoes are tender. 6 to 7 servings.

—Fries with Bacon

Omit butter. Cook 6 thin slices bacon in skillet (see Skillet Cooked Bacon, page 29). Remove crisp bacon, crumble and combine with potatoes. Cook potatoes in the hot bacon drippings.

—Potato-Onion Fry

Peel 2 medium-size onions and cut into thin crosswise rings. Combine with raw sliced potatoes and cook as in Gold Rush Fries or Fries with Bacon.

Barbecued lamb should be served hot. It's not at its best when cold

Outdoor Menu

Dinner in a Boiler

The equipment needed is a clean copper wash boiler and sheets of clean coarse rust-proof screen. The screen is used to separate the layers of food.

The boiler can be set right on your grill. You'll want plenty of hot coals.

The quantities of food used depend upon the size of your boiler, number of guests and the size of their appetites. This recipe is for 8 people.

First layer—Place a long cake rack on bottom of boiler. Put on rack . . .

> *8 potatoes, washed*

Second layer—Remove silk from (do not remove husks) . . .

> *8 ears fresh sweet corn*

Third layer—Clean, rinse and dry with absorbent paper . . .

> *4 broiler chickens, 1 to 1½ lbs. each,*
> *ready-to-cook weight*

Split each chicken in half lengthwise. If chickens are frozen, thaw according to directions on package. Crack joints of drumsticks, hips and wings so chickens can be kept flat. Skewer legs and wings to bodies. Sprinkle each chicken with a mixture of . . .

> 1 *teaspoon salt*
> ½ *teaspoon monosodium glutamate*
> *Dash of pepper*

Place each half on a sheet of heavy aluminum foil with . . .

> 1 *tablespoon butter*

Wrap loosely, closing ends with a double fold.

Fourth layer—Add a layer of . . .

> 4 *live lobsters, freshly killed*
> *(about 1½ lbs. each)*

(See Grilled Lobster, page 34 for directions for killing lobsters and cutting into halves.)

Fifth layer—Scrub and wash in cold running water . . .

> 1 *peck fresh soft clams*

Top off all with . . .

> 1 *lb. butter*
> 3 *large onions, sliced*

and a mixture of . . .

> 1 *cup lemon juice*
> ⅔ *cup (5-oz. bottle) Worcestershire sauce*
> ⅓ *cup salt*
> 3 *tablespoons pepper*
> 4 *bay leaves, crumbled*

Chef's Notes

1. *Tossed Salads* can become your specialty when you add or subtract salad makings. Try Worcestershire sauce, Blue cheese, various herbs, or perhaps some wine vinegars—all to your own taste—using the Caesar Salad recipe.

2. *Hot French Bread*—Wrap in foil and place on grill to heat through before dipping chunks of bread in the butter served with the clams.

3. After a meal such as this, one can only sit back with steaming cups of coffee.

Pour over a mixture of . . .

> 3½ qts. boiling water
> 1 cup wine vinegar
> ¼ cup sugar

Place cover on boiler so that some steam can escape. Place on grill and steam slowly about 2 hrs. Serve this meal in courses, layer by layer. Have a bowl of melted butter to dip clams in. Have plenty for the lobster meat, too. Then, heap your plates with chicken, potatoes and corn.

Caesar Salad

Mix and let stand several hours . . .

> 1 cup olive oil
> 1 clove garlic, crushed

Assemble all ingredients and wash and chill

greens so you can toss the salad with a master's touch the last moment. Heat ¼ cup garlic-flavored oil in skillet. Brown till golden . . .

2 cups small bread cubes

Wash under cold running water and drain well . . .

2 large heads romaine or lettuce

Tear into bite-size pieces and chill. When ready to serve, toss greens with remaining garlic-flavored oil in a large wooden bowl with a mixture of . . .

½ teaspoon salt
¼ teaspoon freshly ground pepper

Break over greens . . .

1 fresh egg (raw)

Pour over egg . . .

Juice of 2 lemons

Toss greens until well coated with egg—they will have a thick creamy coating. Lightly toss greens with browned bread cubes and . . .

½ cup grated Parmesan cheese

Serve immediately. 6 to 8 servings.

—Caesar Salad with Anchovies

Cut 6 fillets of anchovies into bits and mix in with cheese.

Outdoor Menu

Chicken on a Spit

Remove the spit from hooded grill before you build the fire so it won't heat. Clean, rinse and dry with absorbent paper . . .

> *1 chicken, about 4 lbs., ready-to-cook weight*

Rub cavity of bird with about . . .

> *2 teaspoons salt*

Wash, quarter, core and pare . . .

> *2 medium-size apples*

Place in cavity of chicken with . . .

> *1 cup celery leaves, washed*

To close body cavity, sew or skewer and lace with cord. Fasten neck skin to back with skewer. Tie wings to body. Insert spit through chicken. Tie drumsticks to spit by looping cord over tip ends and around spit. Be sure chicken is well balanced. Attach spit; put drip pan in place. Start motor. Baste with . . .

Lemon Basting Sauce (page 8)

Grill about 1½ hrs., or until skin of bird is well browned and begins to split. Baste often to keep skin moist and to add flavor. When using a hand-propelled-type spit, turn bird frequently while roasting. When done, carve and serve with remaining hot sauce. 4 servings.

Fiesta Potato Salad

Toss lightly together with a fork . . .

3 *cups cold, diced, cooked potatoes (see How to Cook Potatoes, page 27)*

⅓ *cup finely sliced scallions (include some sliced green tops)*

6 *slices crisp bacon, crumbled (see Country-Fried Potatoes, page 76)*

2 *tablespoons well-drained slivered pimiento*

1 *teaspoon salt*

½ *teaspoon paprika*

¼ *teaspoon monosodium glutamate*

¼ *teaspoon pepper*

¼ *cup French dressing (with tomato or ketchup base—or perhaps you'd like to use 1 tablespoon vinegar combined with 3 tablespoons bacon drippings)*

Chef's Notes

1. *Spiked Watermelon*—Cut little square plugs in 4 places in the top of an unchilled watermelon; into these insert a brandy-filled corking gun or a strong syringe; squeeze the brandy into the melon slowly so it will absorb the brandy. The melon will take from a pint to a fifth of brandy, depending on its size.

Replace the plugs. Shake melon well, being certain the plugs remain on the upper side so they don't fall out and brandy won't run out.

Place melon on ice to cool; shake it occasionally. Serve the chilled melon in slices.

Cover and chill in mixing bowl for an hour or so. Toss lightly with . . .

> 3 *hard-cooked eggs, sliced*
> ¾ *cup mayonnaise or cooked salad dressing*

Turn into serving bowl. If you want to make a salad look even better, garnish with radishes, tomato wedges, sliced or whole olives or pickle fans. Or plan to outline salad bowl with a border of crisp salad greens. Slide bowl into a plastic bag and chill until ready to serve. 4 to 6 servings.

To Hard-Cook Eggs—Put in a saucepan and cover with cold or lukewarm water . . .

> 3 *eggs*

Cover. Bring water rapidly to boiling. Turn off heat. If necessary to prevent further boiling, remove pan from heat source. Let stand covered about 20 min. Plunge cooked eggs promptly into running cold water. Immediately crackle shells under water. Roll egg between hands to loosen shell. When cooled, start peeling at large end.

Vegetable Cookery for the Grill

Wash fresh vegetables but don't soak them in water for any length of time. Canned or frozen vegetables eliminate preparation and speed your vegetable grill cookery.

COOKING IN KETTLES OR CANS

Perhaps you have special kettles for your outdoor cooking. However, soot will wash off any kettle easily if the outside is rubbed with a moist cake of soap before it is placed on the grill. Or, clean coffee or shortening cans make satisfactory saucepans.

Boiling—Have water boiling rapidly before adding vegetables. Add salt at beginning of cooking period (1 teaspoon per quart of water). After adding vegetables, again bring water to boiling as quickly as possible. Boil at a moderate rate and cook vegetables until just tender. If more water is needed during cooking, add boiling water. In general, cook vegetables covered, in the smallest amount of water possible and for the shortest possible time.

Practice is the best test of how long to cook vegetables.

Heat canned vegetables and their liquid to boiling in kettles or cans. Season with salt, pepper, monosodium glutamate and butter.

Cook frozen vegetables without thawing beforehand. Use as little boiling salt water as possible. Break block apart during cooking. Follow directions on package. Cook vegetables until just tender; season.

Baking—Follow directions in specific recipes.

COOKING IN FOIL

Heavy aluminum foil can be shaped into pots and skillets and used as such.

Break frozen blocks of vegetables into chunks. Place on sheet of heavy aluminum foil. Season with salt, pepper, monosodium glutamate and butter. Shape foil into a loose package, folding edges double. Place package on grill 5 in. from coals, about 5 min. longer than frozen food package directs. Watch carefully and turn occasionally to prevent sticking. Serve vegetables on the foil, edges of foil turned back. Individual packages for each person are attractive and fun.

COOKING ON THE GRILL

Vegetables such as onions, tomatoes, squash and cooked sweet potatoes are listed in various recipes and are cooked directly on the grill. Follow directions with specific recipes.

COOKING ON SKEWERS

See page 47.

COOKING IN THE SKILLET

Vegetables assume new roles when done outdoors even though prepared the same as in the kitchen. When vegetables cook well in a skillet indoors, they cook to perfection in a skillet on the grill. Follow directions with specific recipes.

Hospitality

Section

dips 'n dunks

USE AS DUNKERS: *potato chips, crackers, wafers, pretzels, tortilla chips, corn chips, cucumber slices, celery, carrot and green pepper strips, green onions, cauliflowerets, radishes, pickles, hard roll chunks, toast fingers, french fries, fresh pineapple fingers, apple wedges,* and *shrimp.* Heap Dips and Dunks in bowls with your choice of dunkers around them. Place vegetable dunkers in cracked ice with the bowl of dunk in the center.

Avocado Dunk

Combine . . .

1 *cup mashed avocado*
1 *tablespoon lime or lemon juice*
1 *teaspoon salt*
1 *teaspoon grated onion*

Another time add any one of the following: chopped tomato, chopped ripe olives, crisp crumbled bacon, few drops tabasco sauce, ¼ teaspoon curry powder or 8-oz. pkg. softened cream cheese.

To keep dunk from darkening over a period of time, place a thin layer of mayonnaise over the top. When ready to serve, mix thoroughly.

94

Roquefort or Blue Cheese Dip

Mix thoroughly . . .

  4 oz. crumbled Roquefort or
    Blue cheese
  3-oz. pkg. cream cheese, softened
  1 teaspoon lemon juice
  ½ teaspoon salt

Blend in . . .

  ½ cup whipping cream, whipped

About 2 cups.

Easy-Quick Dips

Whip cheese spreads such as pimiento or bacon with mayonnaise and cream to dunking consistency.

Clam Appetizer Dip

Rub bowl with . . .

  1 clove garlic, cut in half

Cream together in bowl . . .

  2 3-oz. pkg. cream cheese
  1 tablespoon lemon juice
  1 teaspoon Worcestershire sauce
  ½ teaspoon salt
  ⅛ teaspoon ground pepper

Mix in . . .

  1 cup (10 ½-oz. can) chopped
    and drained clams

Thin to dunking consistency with . . .

  Clam broth

About 2 cups.

Snappy Dunk

Blend . . .

  6 oz. smoked or garlic cheese,
    softened
  ½ cup sour cream

Sprinkle with chopped chives.

Cottage Cheese Dips

Blend . . .

  1 cup cottage cheese
  ¼ cup mayonnaise

Combine with any of the following: chopped nuts, olives, chives, onion, green pepper or pimiento, grated Swiss or Cheddar cheese, horseradish, freshly crushed mint leaves or finely chopped celery or parsley.

Pretzel Dunk

Blend . . .

  3-oz. pkg. cream cheese, softened
  ½ cup crushed, drained pineapple

About 1 cup.

Shrimp Dunk

Combine . . .

  1 cup tomato ketchup
  1 tablespoon sugar
  1 tablespoon horseradish
  1 tablespoon lemon juice
  1 teaspoon Worcestershire sauce
  1 teaspoon onion juice
  ½ teaspoon salt
    Few drops tabasco sauce

About 1 cup.

Liver Sausage Dip

Mix . . .

  ¾ cup softened liver sausage
  ¼ cup mayonnaise
  1 tablespoon chopped pickle
  1 teaspoon chopped onion
  ¼ teaspoon salt
  ⅛ teaspoon pepper

About 1 cup.

Fish Dip

Combine . . .

    1 cup flaked cooked salmon, tuna
        or crabmeat
    1 cup cottage cheese
    1/4 cup sour cream
    2 tablespoons chopped pickle
    1 tablespoon lemon juice
    Few drops tabasco sauce

About 2 cups.

Dill Cheese Dip

Mix . . .

    1 cup cottage cheese
    2 teaspoons dill

Let stand overnight. Then serve with tomato wedges and potato chips.

spreads

SET APPETIZER TRAYS where guests can be kept from under foot of the chef but close enough to appreciate his skill in grilling. Spread mixture on several kinds of bases to make an interesting, appetizing tray. Here are some ideas for choice of bases—*bread rounds, squares* or *fingers* of *pumpernickel, rye, wholewheat, white, french, nut* or *raisin; crackers; wafers; melba toast.* For lazy you— fill bowls with spreads. Place bases and spreaders nearby so guests can help themselves. Most spreads can be used as a dunk or dip if thinned with mayonnaise. Prepared cheese or sandwich spreads save time—you simply spread and serve. Here again use your imagination, but to help you start . . .

Special Cheese Spread

Blend well . . .

    3-oz. pkg. cream cheese, softened
    1/4 lb. Blue cheese, crumbled
    3 tablespoons chopped parsley
    2 tablespoons pineapple juice
    1 tablespoon grated onion
    2 tablespoons Worcestershire
        sauce
    1 drop tabasco sauce
    1/2 teaspoon monosodium
        glutamate

About 1 1/2 cups.

Cheese Butter

This is a basic cheese butter which can be used with many adaptations every time you serve appetizers. Blend thoroughly . . .

    1/2 lb. sharp Cheddar or Swiss
        cheese, grated
    1/2 cup cream

Beat in until fluffy . . .

    1 cup softened butter

Add . . .

    1/2 teaspoon salt
    1/8 teaspoon pepper

Then add any one of the following: anchovy paste and Worcestershire sauce, mustard, tarragon vinegar and garlic salt; chopped chives; finely chopped red or green peppers; finely slivered bologna or ready-to-serve meat and prepared mustard; crushed pineapple; diced ham and pickle; chopped pimiento; or crumbled crisp bacon.

Garlic Butter

Crush to a fine paste in a mortar with pestle . . .

>   1 *clove garlic*
>   ¼ *teaspoon salt*

Blend into . . .

>   1 *cup (½ lb.) softened butter*
>   ¼ *cup cream*

Chopped parsley may also be added.

Anchovy Butter

Beat until fluffy . . .

>   1 *cup (½ lb.) softened butter*

Blend in . . .

>   2 *tablespoons anchovy paste*
>   ¼ *teaspoon Worcestershire sauce*

About 1 cup.

Caviar Butter

Beat until fluffy . . .

>   1 *cup (½ lb.) softened butter*

Blend in . . .

>   ¼ *cup caviar*
>   1 *teaspoon onion juice*

About 1¼ cups.

Nut Butter

Beat until fluffy . . .

>   ½ *cup (¼ lb.) softened butter*

Blend in . . .

>   1 *cup ground nuts such as pecans
>   or black walnuts*

About 1½ cups.

Shrimp Paste

This is especially adaptable to the electric blender.

Add to blender in order and blend to a paste . . .

>   1 *tablespoon lemon juice*
>   ½ *teaspoon onion juice*
>   ½ *teaspoon Worcestershire sauce*
>   2 *tablespoons mayonnaise*
>   ½ *lb. cooked shrimp (shelled
>   and deveined)*
>   ¼ *teaspoon salt*

About 1 cup.

Egg Paste

Mash . . .

>   6 *hard-cooked eggs (see* How to
>   Hard-Cook Eggs, page 91).

Whip with . . .

>   ½ *cup mayonnaise*
>   2 *teaspoons grated onion*
>   ½ *teaspoon salt*
>   ½ *teaspoon paprika*
>   ⅛ *teaspoon pepper*

Spread on bases and top with olive slices.

Cress Butter

Wash thoroughly in cold water . . .

1 *bunch water cress*

Chop leaves and blend with . . .

½ *cup butter, softened*

About ¾ cup.

celery stuffers

STUFF CLEANED, crisp celery with mixture, cut into 2-in. lengths and arrange on the appetizer tray. If you have several vegetable relishes try this simple scheme: place vegetables in a wooden bowl with layers of crushed ice (one way to insure crispness throughout the appetizer hour). Around the bowl arrange dunks and celery stuffers. Then let the "helping" guests help themselves. Many of the *Spreads, Dips* or *Dunks* are easy and convenient celery stuffers.

Celery Whirls

When you have time: stuff full length stalks of celery, and put back into natural bunch shape. Wrap tightly in waxed paper and chill for several hours. Cut into thick crosswise slices.

Ham and Cheese Stuffer

Mix . . .

⅓ *cup (3-oz. can) deviled ham*
2 *tablespoons grated sharp cheese*
1 *teaspoon chopped pickle*

Blend in until of spreading consistency . . .

Mayonnaise

About ½ cup.

Blue Cheese Stuffer

Blend . . .

¼ *lb. Blue cheese, crumbled*
3-*oz. pkg. cream cheese, softened*

About ½ cup.

Chutney Stuffer

Blend thoroughly . . .

8-*oz. pkg. cream cheese*
2 *tablespoons cream*
1 *teaspoon curry powder*

Add . . .

¼ *cup chopped Indian Chutney*

Blend and chill. Then stuff celery.

Angels on Horseback

For each appetizer—wrap an oyster in bacon slices. Place on skewer and grill over coals until bacon is done.

Sometimes stick in a rolled anchovy fillet with the oyster.

For other appetizers on skewer *see* Kebabs (page 48-49).

Oysters on the Half Shell

Heap oysters in the half shell on cracked ice. Serve with Shrimp Dunk (page 95).

appetizer cocktails

Serve juices ice cold or, during cool weather, serve vegetable juices steaming hot. Special ice cubes can be made to serve with juices—these will not dilute the cocktail with melting ice. For tomato juice combinations, freeze tomato juice in ice cube tray. And for fruit juice combinations, freeze the principal fruit juice.

Sunshine Cocktail

Place in electric blender container . . .

1 cup water
½ cup diced carrots

Blend until carrots are liquefied. If not using an electric blender, use 1¼ cups carrot juice for carrots and water. Gradually add . . .

4-in. piece celery, chopped
¼ cup diced cucumber
½ cup orange juice
1 tablespoon lime juice
1 tablespoon sugar
1 slice lemon with peel
⅛ teaspoon salt

Blend thoroughly. Serve with lime wedges. 4 servings.

Fruit Juice Cocktail

Combine . . .

2 cups orange juice
2 cups grapefruit juice
1 cup pineapple juice

Chill. Serve in juice glasses with crushed ice and mint sprigs, maraschino cherries or orange or lemon slices. 10 servings.

Cranberry Juice Cocktail

Combine . . .

2 cups cranberry juice
1 cup orange juice
1 cup pineapple juice

Chill. When ready to serve, add . . .

1 qt. gingerale

Serve over crushed ice or topped with orange or lime sherbet. 16 servings.

Seasoned Tomato Juice

Combine until well blended . . .

2 cups tomato juice
1 tablespoon lemon juice
1 teaspoon salt
¼ teaspoon pepper
Few drops tabasco sauce
Dash celery salt

Chill. 4 servings.

Clam-Tomato Cocktail

Mix . . .

2 cups tomato juice
1 cup clam juice
2 teaspoons onion juice
1 teaspoon salt
¼ teaspoon pepper

Chill. Garnish with lemon slices. 6 servings.

beverages hot and cold

Coffee for Forty

Mix thoroughly . . .

1 lb. coffee
2 eggs (and crushed shells)

Tie loosely in fine cheesecloth or put into a lightweight muslin bag. The bag must be large enough to allow the coffee grounds to swell. Put into a large coffee boiler or kettle with . . .

2 gal. freshly drawn water

Cover tightly. Bring slowly to boiling. Boil 3 to 5 min. Taste to test strength. Cover coffee boiler and let stand 10 to 15 min. over low coals or at edge of grill without boiling. 40 servings.

Coffee for Four

Bring to rolling boil . . .

4½ cups cold water

Remove from heat. Add . . .

10 tablespoons coffee

Simmer slowly 8 min. Add . . .

¼ cup cold water
⅛ teaspoon salt

Serve as soon as coffee is clear.

Instant Coffee

Ideal for outdoor serving, concentrated soluble coffee may be prepared with the simple addition of freshly boiling water. Reconstitute concentrated frozen coffee with freshly boiling water. Follow directions on containers.

Iced Coffee

Prepare . . .

Coffee for Forty, for Four or Instant Coffee (use double amount of coffee in all recipes)

Fill tall glasses to brim with . . .

Ice cubes or crushed ice

Pour hot coffee over ice.

Five Ax Tea

For real woodsie flavor, prepare tea in a tin can which you'll keep just for brewing tea.

Bring to boiling in can . . .

   Water

For each cup of water used, add . . .

   2 or 3 teaspoons tea

Cover and let stand about 5 min. Don't wash the soot off the can; the smoky flavor adds much to each succeeding brew. Just rinse out the inside each time.

Tea for Two

Fill serving pot with boiling water. When heated thoroughly, pour off water. Put into pot for each two cups of tea to be brewed . . .

   1 to 2 teaspoons tea

or . . .

   2 prepared tea bags

Pour in . . .

   2 cups freshly boiling water

Cover pot and let tea steep 2 to 5 min. Remove tea bags or strain tea into cups. Serve immediately with lemon.

Iced Tea

Use 1 tablespoon tea per cup of water when preparing Tea for Two or Five Ax Tea. Strain and pour hot tea into pitcher or tall glasses filled with crushed ice or ice cubes.

Minted Iced Tea

Crush 1 or 2 *mint leaves* with 1 *teaspoon sugar* for each glass iced tea. Place in pitcher or glass before adding hot tea.

Chocolate—*Hot and Cold*

Heat together in saucepan over low coals . . .

   2 sq. (2 oz.) unsweetened
      chocolate
   ½ cup water

When chocolate is melted, add . . .

   ¼ cup sugar
   ¼ teaspoon salt

Cook 4 min., stirring constantly. Stir in . . .

   2 cups milk

Heat thoroughly. For a refreshing glass of iced chocolate, cool chocolate and pour over ice cubes or crushed ice in tall glasses. 4 servings.

Cocoa—Hot and Cold

Mix in saucepan . . .

> 5 *tablespoons cocoa*
> 5 *tablespoons sugar*
> *Few grains salt*

Blend in slowly . . .

> 1 *cup water*

Boil gently 2 min. over low coals, stirring until slightly thickened. Move to side of grill. Stir in . . .

> 3 *cups milk*

Heat slowly over hot coals until scalding. Remove from coals. Cover and keep hot at side of grill. Or, cool cocoa and pour over crushed ice cubes or ice in tall glasses. 4 servings.

Lemonade

Squeeze enough lemons for . . .

> ¾ *cup juice (about 4 lemons)*

Mix juice with . . .

> 1 *qt. water*
> 1 *cup Sugar Sirup (page 103)*

Pour over ice cubes or crushed ice in tall glasses. Garnish with mint leaves. Or, dip rims of glasses in lemon juice, then in confectioners' sugar. Let stand a few minutes before adding the iced lemonade. 4 frosty lemonades.

Quick Lemonade

Combine . . .

> ¼ *cup Lemon Sirup (page 103)*
> ½ *cup water*

Pour over ice cubes or crushed ice in a tall glass. 1 quick lemonade.

Mulled Cider

Bring to boiling in saucepan . . .

> 2 *qts. cider*

Tie in cheesecloth bag and add to cider . . .

> 1½ *teaspoons whole cloves*
> 5 *small sticks cinnamon*
> 5 *whole allspice*

Boil 3 min. Cool and remove spice bag. When ready to serve, bring again to boiling and serve at once. Garnish with unpared red apple rings stuck with whole cloves.

Sparkling Lemonade

Pour into quart container . . .

> 1 *5- or 6-oz. can lemonade*
> *concentrate*

Fill container with . . .

> *Gingerale, chilled*

Pour over ice cubes or crushed ice in tall glasses. 4 sparkling servings.

Limeade

Prepare *Limeade* the same as *Lemonade*, substituting the juice of fresh limes for lemons or lime concentrate for lemon.

Peppermint Malt

Prepare peppermint sirup by scalding in double boiler . . .

> 4 *cups milk*

Add . . .

    ½ cup crushed peppermint
      stick candy

Stir or shake until dissolved. Chill.

For malt, add to cold sirup . . .

    ¾ cup malted milk powder
    6 scoops ice cream

Mix in shaker or electric blender.
Pour into 6 tall glasses.

Chocolate Malt

Mix . . .

    1 cup milk
    2 tablespoons malted milk
      powder
    2 tablespoons chocolate sirup

Beat with rotary beater or mix in
shaker or electric blender until frothy.
Add . . .

    1 or 2 scoops softened ice cream

Beat until well blended. Pour into
tall glass.

Milk Shakes

Any of the recipes for *Malts* can be
used for *Milk Shakes*. Simply omit
the malted milk powder. For a lighter
drink, omit ice cream.

Chocolate Soda

Combine . . .

    1 cup milk
    ½ cup gingerale or carbonated
      water
    2 tablespoons chocolate sirup

Pour into tall glass. Add . . .

    1 scoop vanilla or chocolate
      ice cream

Serve at once.

Strawberry Soda

Pour into a tall glass . . .

    1 cup bottled strawberry soda
      beverage

Add . . .

    1 or 2 scoops vanilla or
      strawberry ice cream

Or, mash enough berries for ⅓ cup
crushed strawberries. Place in glass
with 1 cup carbonated water. Add ice
cream and serve.

Black Cow

Place in tall glass . . .

    1 or 2 scoops vanilla ice cream

Fill glass with . . .

    Root beer

Try bottled cola or soda beverages in
place of root beer for variety of floats.

Sugar Sirup

Mix in saucepan . . .

    2 cups sugar
    2 cups water

Cover, bring to boiling and boil 5
min. Cool and store in refrigerator.
Use this as a base for all the "ades"
and many of the recipes in the *Alco-
holic Drinks* section, following. 2½
cups sirup.

Lemon Sirup

Combine . . .

    2 cups lemon juice
    1½ cups sugar
    1½ tablespoons grated lemon peel

Store in refrigerator. 1 pt. sirup.

jigger	1 ½ oz.
pony	¾ oz.
dash	6 drops or 1/10 teaspoon

alcoholic drinks

Gin Buck

Pour into 10-oz. glass, juice of . . .
   ½ lemon
Drop peel from squeezed lemon half into glass. Add . . .
   1 jigger dry Gin
   Ice cubes (1 or 2)
Fill glass with . . .
   Gingerale
Stir and serve. A *Rum Buck* is made by substituting *Puerto Rican Rum* for the Dry Gin.

Applejack Cobbler

Fill goblet or 10-oz. glass half full with . . .
   Ice, finely crushed
Pour over ice . . .
   1 teaspoon confectioners' sugar
   1 ½ jiggers Applejack
Stir until outside of glass is covered with frost. Insert straws and decorate glass with orange and pineapple slices. For a *Brandy Cobbler*, substitute Brandy for the Applejack.

Gin Cobbler

Fill goblet or 10-oz. glass half full with . . .
   Ice, finely crushed
Pour over ice . . .
   1 teaspoon confectioners' sugar
   1 ½ jiggers dry Gin
Stir until outside of glass is coated with frost. Insert straws and decorate glass with orange and pineapple slices.

Rum Cobbler

Fill goblet or 10-oz. glass half full with . . .
   Ice, finely crushed
Pour over ice . . .
   ⅓ teaspoon Curaçao
   1 jigger New England Rum
Stir until outside of glass is coated with frost. Insert straws and decorate glass with orange slices.

Whiskey Cobbler

Fill goblet or 10-oz. glass half full with . . .
   Ice, finely crushed
Pour over ice . . .
   1 teaspoon confectioners' sugar
   1 ½ jiggers Rye Whiskey
Stir until outside of glass is coated with frost. Insert straws and decorate glass with orange and pineapple slices.

Sherry Wine Cobbler

Fill goblet or 10-oz. glass half full with : .

Ice, finely crushed

Pour over ice and twist lemon peel . . .

1 teaspoon confectioners' sugar
Sherry Wine to fill glass

Stir until outside of glass is coated with frost. Insert straws and decorate glass with orange and pineapple slices.

Alexander Cocktail

Combine . . .

1 jigger Brandy or Dry Gin
1 jigger heavy cream
1 jigger Creme de Cocoa

Shake well with crushed ice. Strain into cocktail glass.

Bacardi Cocktail

Combine . . .

1 jigger Bacardi Rum
Juice of 1 lime
1 teaspoon Grenadine

Shake well with crushed ice. Strain into Cocktail glass.

Bourbon Cocktail

Combine . . .

1 pony Benedictine
1 pony Bourbon Whiskey
2 teaspoons lemon juice
½ teaspoon Curaçao
2 dashes Angostura Bitters

Shake well with crushed ice. Strain into cocktail glass.

Brandy Cocktail

Combine . . .

1 jigger Brandy
2 dashes Angostura Bitters
½ teaspoon Sugar Sirup (pg. 103)

Add crushed ice; stir well. Strain into cocktail glass. Add twist of lemon peel.

Mint Julep

Crush in bottom of 12-oz. glass . . .

4 or 6 mint leaves

Half fill glass with shaved ice. Add . . .

4 or 6 mint leaves, crushed

Fill glass with shaved ice. Set in refrigerator to frost outside of glass. Meanwhile, blend in mixing glass . . .

2 jiggers Bourbon Whiskey
2 teaspoons Sugar Sirup (pg. 103)

Pour slowly over ice in prepared Julep glass. Add more shaved ice to mound glass. Decorate with mint sprig dipped in confectioners' sugar.

Daiquiri Cocktail

Combine . . .

2 teaspoons Sugar Sirup
  (page 103)
2 teaspoons lime juice
1 jigger Puerto Rican Rum

Shake well with crushed ice. Strain into chilled cocktail glass.

For a *Frozen Daiquiri*, double ingredients, use twice as much ice, place in electric blender and blend until Daiquiri is consistency of snow.

Manhattan Cocktail

Combine . . .

1 *jigger Whiskey*
1 *pony Italian Vermouth*
1 *dash Angostura Bitters*

Stir well with ice cubes. Strain into cocktail glass. Add . . .

Maraschino cherry·

Serve at once.

Martini Cocktail (Dry)

Combine . . .

1 *jigger Dry Gin*
½ *pony French Vermouth*

Stir well with ice cubes. Strain into chilled cocktail glass. Twist lemon peel for oil on surface. Add . . .

Olive

Serve at once.

Old-Fashioned Cocktail

Blend in Old-Fashioned glass . . .

1 *teaspoon Sugar Sirup*
(page 103)
2 *dashes Angostura Bitters*

Stir in . . .

1 *pony Bourbon Whiskey*

Add . . .

1 *or 2 cracked ice cubes*
1 *jigger Bourbon Whiskey*

Stir and add . . .

Twist lemon peel
Maraschino cherry
½ *orange slice*

Serve at once.

Side Car Cocktail

Frost rim of cocktail glass by rubbing with a piece of cut lemon and dipping in confectioners' sugar.

Combine in equal parts . . .

Lemon juice
Cointreau
Brandy

Shake well with cracked ice. Strain into frosted cocktail glass.

Vodka Cocktail

Combine . . .

1 *jigger Vodka*
1 *pony lemon or lime juice*
1 *dash Grenadine*
⅓ *teaspoon Angostura or Orange Bitters*

Shake well with crushed ice. Strain into cocktail glass.

Tom Collins

Combine . . .

1½ *jiggers Old Tom Gin*
Juice of 1 medium lemon or lime
1 *teaspoon confectioners' sugar*

Stir in Collins glass. Add . . .

3 *or 4 ice cubes*
Carbonated water (to fill glass)

Stir quickly. If Dry Gin is used, double amount of sugar.

Apricot Cooler

Combine . . .

1 jigger Apricot Brandy
Juice of half a lemon
Juice of half a lime
2 dashes of Grenadine

Shake well with cracked ice. Strain into Collins glass. Add . . .

Ice cubes
Carbonated water

Decorate glass with orange or lemon.

Horse's Neck Highball

Combine in highball glass . . .

1 jigger dry Gin
2 ice cubes
Gingerale (to fill glass)

Cut spiral of lemon peel and hook over edge of glass.

Whiskey Highball

Combine in highball glass . . .

1 jigger Rye, Bourbon or Scotch
Whisky
2 ice cubes
Gingerale or carbonated water
(to fill glass)

Stir and serve at once.

Silver Gin Fizz

Combine . . .

1 jigger dry Gin
Juice of ½ lemon
1 teaspoon Sugar Sirup
(page 103)
1 egg white

Shake vigorously 3 to 5 min. with crushed ice. Strain into chilled 8-oz. glass. Fizz with . . .

Carbonated water (to fill glass)

Stir quickly.

Planters Punch

This can be made for any number and is served in Collins glasses. The formula is world famous as 1-2-3.

1 part Sugar Sirup (page 62)
2 parts lemon or lime juice
3 parts Jamaica Rum
2 dashes Angostura Bitters

Shake well with crushed ice, pour into glass packed with crushed ice. Place in refrigerator until glasses begin to frost. Decorate with pineapple, lime or what you will.

Index